T0064148

LIFE
of
CHARLIE

CHARLES HUNT

PARTRIDGE
A Penguin Random House Company

Copyright © 2014 by Charles Hunt.

ISBN: Hardcover   978-1-4828-9558-2
           Softcover   978-1-4828-9556-8
           Ebook   978-1-4828-9240-6

All rights reserved. No part of this book may be used or reproduced by any means, graphic, electronic, or mechanical, including photocopying, recording, taping or by any information storage retrieval system without the written permission of the publisher except in the case of brief quotations embodied in critical articles and reviews.

Because of the dynamic nature of the Internet, any web addresses or links contained in this book may have changed since publication and may no longer be valid. The views expressed in this work are solely those of the author and do not necessarily reflect the views of the publisher, and the publisher hereby disclaims any responsibility for them.

To order additional copies of this book, contact
Toll Free 800 101 2657 (Singapore)
Toll Free 1 800 81 7340 (Malaysia)
orders.singapore@partridgepublishing.com

www.partridgepublishing.com/singapore

"AUGUSTA. Western Australia.
This is where the Author lives in retirement. A touch of Paradise."

CONTENTS

RETIREMENT

They say these are the best years of your life and they're more than likely right. There's very little stress and you can stay in bed if you wish. This is something that never really interested me and I can't think of one day of my life that I've slept in after 7am.

I've loved my work and have been self-employed for most of my working life. When I've tired of one venture, I've moved onto the next. The last venture, however, made me realise that I was working for the wrong reason.

It was a seafood restaurant in Margaret River, a town voted by Lonely Planet as one of the top ten places in the world. However, I didn't see much of it as I was too busy working. One day I realised I was working and stressing for one reason, to make sure my staff had a job. My son Graeme, who was now helping me, said "let's get the hell out of here and go fishing". Graeme, for all his faults, was a fairly smart person, he lived life how he liked it. His motto was "have a good time but don't hurt anyone in the process". He was also a very good worker who always put in a full day.

So, I've retired. First, move to a fishing village and buy a boat. I need to map out a plan as sometimes the fish don't bite or the weather is bad, so we need a Plan B. Gardening, yes that seems like a good Plan B. Plan C will be community work, I can give something back to those who need it and Plan D will be travel. I've always travelled and now I have time to do some more. Four Plans should keep me occupied and I can fill in any spare time golfing. This is something I can do with Graeme, as Augusta has a lovely nine hole golf course as well as a full 18 hole course.

There is not a lot of employment in Augusta but Graeme is picking up work here and there. He has four part-time jobs going—fishing with a commercial fisherman, working at a local caravan park, spending two days a week looking after a disabled boy and sometimes helping out of a night at the local fish and chip shop. Any spare time he has, we go fishing or golfing. This is the life.

Plan B—Gardening

My father was a great gardener. My first memories of Dad were growing vegetables to sell and help support his family. In his retirement years, he built a glasshouse and raised orchids. Unfortunately, I didn't take a lot of interest in the orchids as I was in my teenage years and there were a lot more exciting things to do so sadly I didn't inherit my father's gardening genes. I have enjoyed growing vegetables at various times in my life with little success. My retirement gardening is mainly herbs and small shrubs in pots. Strawberries, blueberries and raspberries, this is hardly enough to keep me busy but easy on my aging back and knees.

Plan C—Community Work

I deliver meals on wheels and enjoy it. I was driving for the hospital, taking patients to Busselton for treatment. The trouble with being a volunteer is the same as being a charity donor, donate to one charity and a dozen others jump on board. The same thing happened with the hospital. They had me taking patients out for a drive, a day out for them but sometimes I had other fish to fry, such as watching my football team. I now donate to charities in an anonymous capacity.

Plan D—Travel

I've always been interested in travelling. The best way to educate yourself is to travel. Travel anywhere, the next town, the next state, another country, it doesn't really matter.

I had already visited a lot of countries. I've been to most Asian countries, the west coast of the United States, spent some time in New Zealand and now I could go anywhere that pleased me. My sister Lea has talked about Turkey so that would be the first on my list. Gaye wasn't well enough or interested in travelling so I went it alone and joined a tour group. I thought that would be more fun, it was and I met some wonderful people. Some of them like Katherine, Merryn and Dave are still good friends.

Next was Morocco and France with sister Lea. This was my next major trip. It was exciting and a good bonding exercise with my sister. I had a good time apart from the fact I nearly died from a kidney infection, I picked up in Morocco.

I then went cruising with my other sister Glen and brother-in-law Murray. First to New Zealand, this was a great trip. The first time cruising is exciting and it was also more than that because it was with my family. Next time I go cruising it would be around Australia. I'm not sure if I'll travel anymore. Air travel used to be fun, now it sucks, big time! Being herded along like cattle, strip searched by the "Gestapo", made to unpack your bags in front of everyone in Paris just because the snarly woman thought I was English. Yeah, that wasn't too good, put me right off. Then once on the aircraft, you are cooped up like sardines for maybe up to 15 hours. Then getting seated next to someone who was anywhere like normal is like winning lotto.

Of course, you don't have to travel overseas. But I also covered this fairly well by driving my 4WD all around Australia. I have visited and explored just about all of Australia. So will I travel anymore? I'm not sure, I've seen just about every country of interest to me. I've also been to Mauritius, yeah forgot about Mauritius, been there, done that.

Living in the best place in the best country in the world, why would I want to go anywhere else? Canada, Alaska and New York, still interest me. Why New York? I'm not sure but I think I would like it. Canada and Alaska, well they just speak for themselves. So if I don't travel and don't fish (my fishing partner is no longer with us so I don't do a lot of fishing lately), the gardening is well under control, it doesn't take much time and community work is just meals on wheels so that isn't time consuming so WHAT DO I DO WITH MYSELF NOW?? You may well laugh but I'm going to write a book, an autobiography.

Who would be interested enough to even read it? Doesn't matter, makes it easier to write if I'm the only one who's going to read it, it can be as boring as all hell. Who cares, I will love it! I have a good memory but no idea how to write a book, no idea how to construct it, not all that good at spelling or grammar. I have a good imagination though but this book will be factual. The one and only rule—stick to the facts!

CHAPTER 1

GROWING UP

Red Cliffs

As I said before, I have a fairly good memory and I can even remember my early years. Born on 29 December 1936 in Red Cliffs, Victoria, to parents Rupert and Phyllis Hunt, I had a very good, stable upbringing.

Red Cliffs is a small country town in the north west of Victoria on the mighty Murray River, about 25 kms from the regional city of Mildura. I was the middle child, having a big sister, Lea, and a younger sister Glenys. Rupert and Phyllis were supportive and loving parents. I think I may have inherited Dad's genes, as we both love to be self-employed. He came from a farming background and my first memories of him were his poultry farm and vegetable garden. Throughout his life he was always employed and could turn his hand to most things. Mum was a very good mother, caring and supportive, maybe living a little in the background, but after Dad's death she flourished and we saw a new side to her. She took up painting, dancing and came out of her shell. She lived a long life and died in her 90s.

But back to me, my first memories were when I was around two years old. Some people say this is highly unlikely. "Too young to remember anything", they say "you are dreaming". I can remember my sister Glen, sleeping as a baby in her cot in my parent's room. There is 18 months difference in our ages so I must've been quite young. Lea and I slept in a sleep out adjoining their room and we had to keep quiet so as not to disturb the new baby.

Our weatherboard house was very small and basic but comfortable and to us, it was a happy, normal house of those times. Nearly 60 years later, I went back to Red Cliffs and visited my school and found to my surprise that our house was still there. It was somewhat different, larger with some obvious renovations. It was the location that made it great. Set in the middle of a vineyard, with an orange grove on one side and a small forest out the front which we had to cross to walk to school. There was an irrigation channel out the front as well which is now covered by a sealed road.

Red Cliffs is a large grape, citrus and walnut growing area, literally carved out of the desert. The region is irrigated by a system of channels sourced from the Murray River, without this water not much would grow as the yearly rainfall is very low. We had a poultry farm out the back, along with a vegetable garden and out the front we had a cow. Yes, fresh milk and cream, eggs and vegetables, no wonder we were healthy kids. Our house consisted of only one bedroom, with a big sleep out at the front, a kitchen, bathroom and living room and that was it. Apart from the toilet which was a freestanding little house in the backyard, this was the norm in those days.

Charles at 20 months in Red Cliffs

Mum with baby Glen, Lea and me.
Red Cliffs house

We three kids slept in the sleep out that was of course, when Glen was old enough to graduate from her cot. No TV in those days, so we gathered around the radio after dinner to listen to the serials. Search for the Golden Boomerang and Biggles were among the regular ones, then it was off to bed. We would discuss the day's events and chatter away until Mum and Dad went to bed. We would be told to be quiet and go to sleep after which we would continue on in whispers. Eventually we would go to sleep but not until each of us said "I am going to sleep now and never wake up until the morning". This is indelibly seared in my brain as we must've said it thousands of times, it was like a ritual. It was a bit like the TV Walton's saying goodnight to each other and then the lights going out one by one. Maybe they pinched this idea from us? Maybe not!

My preschool years were pretty much spent tied to my mother's apron strings, I wasn't very adventurous and maybe I didn't like sharing the limelight with my little sister. I used to be the youngest and, I guess, the centre of attention and I remember one of our first trips to the shops, Glen was to ride in a pusher and I was to walk, I soon put a stop to that by stacking on a real turn outside the shop, Glen vacated the pusher and I moved in, she then stood by the pusher telling me Mummy wouldn't be long. She would've been three, maybe four. From then on I had the upper hand, I could just about get her to do anything. She was fairly adventurous. She nearly cut off her fingers when I talked her into operating the chaff cutter. Then there was the time I dared her to climb up onto the roof of the fruit drying racks. This was very high. She was running up and down and Mum and Dad were traumatised and not too sure how to get her down. She was in big trouble.

I can remember, one Sunday morning all dressed up for Sunday school and playing outside on the plank which crossed the irrigation channel as a bridge. I fell off into the fast-flowing current and surely would've drowned, only for the fact that my sisters fished me out. The up side to this was no Sunday School for me that day. We only had one

Sunday best outfit so I had the day off. This experience had a major impact on me a little bit later.

I had long, blonde, curly hair which Mum brushed and combed lovingly. Dad took control and said it was time to get rid of it. No doubt thinking that it might toughen me up, make a man of me, big mistake! When the barber sat me on a box in his chair and got out his scissors, I stacked on a real show, one of my better performances. I think Dad was so embarrassed that he never mentioned my hair again.

When I went back to Red Cliff, nearly 60 years later, I sat in the same chair and had another haircut. The shop was still there and the guy said it was probably his grandfather who cut my hair all those years ago as the shop had been in the family all that time. Red Cliffs in general hadn't changed all that much. It was like it was in a time warp.

School

Exciting stuff this school, loved it, until Mum said goodbye, she was leaving, I would be on my own! Like hell, I wasn't having any of that, I was traumatised. Mum was recalled to sit in with me until I settled down. Yeah, she could stay all day, it was fun! They tried to wean me off again, didn't work, so they put Plan B into operation and brought big sister Lea out of her class. This worked, I was happy, it was explained that one day she would have to go back to own class, OK with me, maybe when I was in Grade 2 she could leave, that would be fine. This was getting ugly, I was lonely, the other kids didn't seem to like me, the teacher was very tricky but I was awake up to her, I would make her life hell, she would then have to send me home. You may think I was a spoiled, sooky little brat but you must remember that I had been raised on a farm and had never seen any other kids, let alone played with them, apart from my sisters of course. It was daunting and nothing like I had imagined school would be like. No TV in those days so I had no idea what to expect. My sisters have always insisted that I was the favourite child, especially with Dad. I'm not sure what they are on about, though I was fairly cute so maybe I deserved a bit of special attention. "You've never done the dishes" they say, I'm sure that's not true and anyway that's girls work! Anyway I do plenty of dishes these days, I have no choice.

Days went by, maybe weeks, it was the worst time of my life, then an angel appeared, in the form of Miss Bates, she was to be the new teacher. I'm not sure what happened to the other one maybe she was having a nervous breakdown? Who cared? Miss Bates understood me, she was young, this was probably her first posting and she was out to impress. We immediately bonded, she sat me up the front of the class, where she could give me special attention. Occasionally slipping me the odd lolly or two when no-one was watching. She knew how to treat a man. I was a model child, no more tantrums, it was a case of you scratch my back and I'll scratch yours. Miss Bates was a legend and no doubt, in the running for teacher of the year. She had tamed the monster.

An example of her work was when the class had to go for swimming lessons. We had to walk about 2kms from the school to the pool which was in town. She held my hand on the walk. Well we had to cross the main road and she didn't want her star pupil to be run over! The last little bit of the walk was too much for me so she piggybacked me, to hell with what the other kids thought, I couldn't care less. Then the shock came. We actually had to get into the water! I was having none of that, you could drown in there! Miss Bates assured me she would look after me and said "look at all the other kids, they are having so much fun". I couldn't care less, I wasn't going in and that was that!

Eventually she saw reason and said "Charles, you don't have to go in if you don't want to and if you stop crying I will get a treat for you". She took me over to the kiosk and bought us both an ice-cream. We sat on the bench side by side and watched the smiles disappear from the faces of the losers in the pool. I guess my fear of the water was due to the former instance in the irrigation channel when my sisters had to fish me out. How Miss Bates was able to figure that one out was a mystery. Luckily my fear of the water was conquered in later years, I certainly didn't pass this fear onto my children, and certainly not my grandsons.

Tragedy was to strike some weeks later. Miss Bates' stupid boyfriend crashed his motorbike and she received a badly broken leg. She did come back to school some months later but was assigned to the office as she was on crutches for some time.

The rest of my Red Cliff's schooling was fairly uneventful, it was hard to play cute during maths and science and if you threw a tantrum you would cop a good clip around the ear. This was the era when teachers were able to torture their students. Their weapon of choice was a strap. They would dish out six of the best. Our Technical Drawing teacher was a dab hand at a T-square, a couple of whacks around your backside was even worse than the strap. At least with the strap you could always plead that your hand was too sore to write. This would bring a grin to the torturer who would be satisfied with his work although sometimes you would cop a couple more on the other hand just to even it up.

Later on at Preston Tech I discovered two of the all time great torturers, as far as strap wielders go. There was our Maths teacher, Zombie Meehan and the English teacher, Mr Ali Barbar. Zombie could be compared to Fonzie in Happy Days, no-one ever saw him in action, he didn't need to get physical as his reputation and presence always did the trick. A click of his fingers was all he needed. No-one in our class had ever seen him in action but the rumour was that he could virtually put you in hospital if he wanted to.

Zombie always made a dramatic entrance into the classroom. He would open the door, take one step inside, pause, staring straight ahead. It was a bit like a maestro making his entrance, stepping up onto the rostrum before a concert. Pausing then bowing. We would half expect Zombie to bow but that would be most inappropriate for a Zombie. Instead he would walk to his desk in long, slow strides, staring straight ahead, the only thing missing was holding his arms out zombie fashion. He would then open the top drawer of his desk, take out his two metre or so long strap and put it out on top of the desk and then roll it up. He would then place it in an easy to reach location on his desk, all the time still staring straight ahead. You could well imagine he could do this in his sleep. We would be mesmerised, even though we had seen this ritual performed many times before. Zombie didn't speak much, he would usually just write a number on the blackboard and this would be the page in our text book that he wanted us to complete. We knew the procedure so we went to work immediately. Zombie had super powers and we knew it.

Ali Barbar was as different as chalk is to cheese from Zombie, Ali was a talker, well he was the English teacher I suppose, and he would bounce around in front of the class firing questions at a rapid rate. If he didn't get a quick reply he would sometimes pull you out in front of the class for your share of capital punishment, well corporal punishment maybe. Now Ali wasn't a big man, he had a round head and wore small, round rimless glasses. He looked just like Tojo. For those who aren't familiar with Tojo he was the supreme commander of the Japanese Armed Forces during the war, he was despised nearly as much as Hitler and was executed as a war criminal after the war.

We, however, never wanted Ali to be executed, he was too much fun. Being fairly short in stature, he would jump off the ground when wielding the strap, he must've thought this would give him maximum impact. However, most times it would just interfere with his aim and he would completely miss the target altogether. This would infuriate him and he would blame the victim for pulling his hand away. Sometimes it was tempting to deliberately do this as he might hit his own leg with the follow through. This would bring cheers from the class. The cheers would be somewhat muffled because if he thought you were making a fool of him, which wasn't hard to do, you would be next in line. Usually the whole thing would just turn into a pantomime and Ali would get somewhat disorientated and not be too sure who he had strapped and who he hadn't. Both Zombie and strap happy Ali should be in the Hall of Fame, they are legends.

In order to avoid the strap I would have to change my tactics, bring another entirely new game plan into play. Make myself invisible.

To do this you had to pick a desk on the side and somewhere halfway down the class. The kids at the front and the back seemed to cop all the attention but I would blend in with the walls. Never volunteer to answer a question, never make eye contact with the teacher and always have your homework up to scratch, this way you never got called up in front of the class and made an example of.

I was a fairly good student, not brilliant but not dumb. This suited my strategy, the teacher hardly knew I was there at all, I was good at most subjects although algebra was my downfall, it was like a language from another planet. Sports day was always good, I could run fast and was the school champion for my age, this took a lot of pressure off, I even think some of the other kids were beginning to like me. Dad seemed proud and that made me feel good.

Camping on the river Murray with Dad

Occasionally, usually on a Friday, my sister Lea would call into my class and hand the teacher a note, I was wanted at home, it was urgent. I knew what it was, we were going fishing and camping on the Murray River! Dad was an expert fisherman and always caught fish, Murray Cod and Red Fin Perch were the usual catch. We had a tent and a campfire and I was allowed to drink billy tea, this was tea boiled in a billy. The billy was a metal container with a lid on it. Billy tea is the best tea you can get, the taste brewed over an open fire is altogether different to today's tea. We cooked the fish, and made a damper. Sometimes Dad shot a rabbit, he was an excellent marksman and won many awards at local shows. He may have passed this onto my son Graeme who was fascinated with my guns. Years later when I set off on my own, Dad gave me his favourite rifle which I still have.

There wasn't a lot happening in Red Cliffs but most of us kids didn't mind. I would visit my pal Edwin Goodison who lived up the road. He had a huge Mulberry Tree in his backyard, we would spend half the day up there in a cubby house, coming home with blue mulberry stains all over our faces and clothes.

The war was on and the real threat was that Japan was going to invade Australia, they were already bombing Darwin and Broome, we had air raid drill at school, we would have to put on gas masks and climb into trenches. The people next door to us had dug an air raid shelter we were invited to use it if the need arose. It didn't luckily.

Another exciting event was the night when the packing sheds burnt down. The packing sheds was a factory where they packed the dried fruit, sultanas, currants and raisins. It has been rebuilt now and it produces most of Australia's dried fruit under the brand name of Sunbeam. This was a big event. It happened around dinner time and I can remember Glen and I running barefoot to get a look. The factory wasn't far from our place and the whole town were there trying to put it out. Mum and Dad let us stay up very late as the town was in shock, a lot of people would lose their jobs.

Pretty soon Mum had a brilliant idea, she could tell I was a very sensitive person and thought therefore, I might be musical. She bought a banjo and make a beautiful maroon velvet cover for it. Banjos are easy to play and once I mastered that I could move onto something more complex. I was sent off to lessons in town and everyone had high hopes. Mum played the piano so we might turn out to be a real family act. After some weeks I was coming along nicely, I could manage the first couple of bars of Twinkle, Twinkle Little Star. It was about this time that I hit a bit of a road block. Twinkle, Twinkle wasn't improving so the teacher tried other tunes. She expected me to read sheet music, I had no idea. It looked a cross between algebra and Chinese to me. I had to up the ante with my practice, two hours after school, with Mum showing lots of patience. The banjo had cost a lot of money to Mum but never mind they might be able to find someone else to offload it to and maybe get their money back. Dad was on my side, and said "how would you like to join the Police Boys Club and do sports?". Yes! Anything to get rid of that bloody banjo.

I was to do boxing, I might be good at it, training was good, I felt good but who was I going to fight? I was the youngest and the smallest at the Club. Which was the worst, the dreaded banjo or being smashed in the face every week? But at least I got better at boxing. I must've joined at a time when all the kids were semi-professionals. Later on some new kids joined, they were more my style, and I even won a few bouts.

Big changes were coming, the war had ended and we were off to Melbourne to live. Mum and Dad had bought a business in North Carlton, a Milk Bar/Deli type shop. All our animals had to go, Barney our horse, Sam our dog and hundreds of chooks. Glen and I were to go to Lee St State School which was only a block or two away from the shop. I was sad to go, I was just starting to blossom and I was allowed to go to the pictures of a Saturday afternoon and we used to sit in those long deck chair type things. The battle to get the front row was always on and Judith Allen seemed to end up sitting next to me. Serials were on every week and they were not to be missed, Tom Mix, Hopalong Cassidy, The Lone Ranger and a couple of monster type movies.

We travelled Melbourne by steam train, we were used to this type of travel as holidays were spent mainly in Ballarat where our grandparents lived. The train line wasn't far away from our house and just at the back of the school. I wasn't to return to Red Cliffs for nearly 60 years.

Carlton

We were in for a major culture shock. Coming from a peaceful small town to the big inner city was an eye opener. The war had ended and there was mass unemployment. North Carlton was one of the roughest, toughest places in Australia. Our shop was very busy. Lea was working with Mum and Dad, while Glen and I started school. I seemed to fit in fairly well and the majority of kids were very poor. I always had an endless supply of lollies which made me very popular.

I had one year of primary school and then off to high school. I attended Collingwood Technical School, catching two buses to get there. It was a bit daunting at first but I soon adapted. I enjoyed the freedom. Mum and Dad were very busy in the shop and most times I had free reign. I soon learnt the rules to surviving in that jungle. You have to join in. A lot of the kids didn't even have shoes and I saw poverty first hand. Some of my mates had parents that were drunk nearly all the time. It was so sad but being a kid, it didn't really worry me, it was just all part of the times. I sold newspapers on Friday and Saturday nights, dodging in and out of the traffic as the cars stopped at the traffic lights. My parents would've had a fit if they'd known, they thought I was safe at home or at a friend's place.

I soon learnt to fight. Being small and somewhat of a privileged kid, in their eyes anyway, I suppose I was the target for bullies. I handled that by getting in first. Bullies don't like their own medicine and are generally cowards. No turning the other cheek for me, they would've just belted that one as well.

Dad and I would go to every Collingwood football game, this was when I learnt to love Aussie Rules football. Saturdays were Dad's day off and I knew every Collingwood player and one day dreamed of playing with them. Little did I know, I would come close to realising that dream—not all that close, but fairly close. I will cover this in another chapter.

One of my worst memories of the Carlton days was the dentist, this was a major trauma. My first teeth refused to come out and my second teeth were on the scene and crowding my mouth. I guess this was because of our early healthy and high calcium diet. My bones have always been very strong, the downside was that I had to have 15 teeth out—all in one hit. I was put to sleep with chloroform and tasted that awful stuff for years to come. Every time I visited a dentist in following years, the trauma returned.

Day at the beach in Carlton days

Thank goodness this wasn't very often as my teeth are very healthy, even to this day. I had my first dental work done only last year after 40 years of avoiding dentists. Removal of wisdom teeth and the capping of a couple of chipped teeth was all I needed. The dentist was amazed!

After nearly two years in Carlton, Mum and Dad had had enough, working days and nights, seven days a week was too much for anyone. I was to get to know this feeling later in life when I owned my own small businesses. Mum's parents were in poor health and they were getting old, so it was decided we would relocate to Ballarat to be closer to them.

Ballarat

Our house in Ballarat was of weatherboard construction, comfortable but not really suitable for Ballarat's cold weather. Ballarat is Australia's equivalent to the United State's Minnesota as far as weather goes.

There were strong family ties on both sides of our parents in the town and I have many memories of Ballarat due to our numerous visits. One of these memories is of all of us sleeping in the living room as this was the only room with heating. Dad would light a fire in the open fireplace and we would all bring our beds in. We would have so many blankets on we could hardly move. Bed socks were a must and we all had chilblains. Never had these before and never since, but Ballarat was capable of bringing out this strange, itchy, annoying condition. The best part of this dwelling was that it was on a large block with plenty of room to play, more like our life in Red Cliffs. In Carlton we lived on top of the shop and only had a tiny backyard.

The downside to this house was that we had a witch living next door. Yes, a real, live witch, or so our new friends said! How good was this? Not really, it was downright scary actually! Rhoda was her name and sometimes she would stand on her side of the fence and beckon us to come over, we would run like hell. Her house was like you see in the movies, you know, the haunted variety, all broken down with lots of high weeds. Sometimes Dad would talk to her and we believed this was just a plot on her behalf to get her hands on us. We would have none of that and made sure we didn't play on her side of the yard. Lose your ball in her yard and it was gone forever. It never really occurred to us that she might just be a lonely old lady. Anyway, it was a bit exciting at the time.

I was to attend the Ballarat School of Mines, this was just a fancy name for a Technical College. Ballarat has a rich history in gold mining and now has an historical village where tourists can go and see what life was like 150 years ago.

My most vivid memory was one morning when it was snowing and my old pushbike was broken. Kenny Rouse, my best friend, offered to dink me to school. No parent lifts to school in cars in those days, you got there the best way you could. Ballarat is very hilly and Kenny was struggling, but I hardly noticed, or cared. At least he was warm, being on the front of the bike, I was snap frozen and how I didn't have hypothermia I don't know. I had to be chiselled off the bike covered in snow. Gloves, six or seven pullovers and a raincoat were no match for Ballarat.

I needed a new bike and put it to Dad. He would come to the party but I had to work for it. My first job would be delivering newspapers before school. Dad had arranged the job for me. I would have to cycle to the train station, this was a fair distance but not to worry, I had a full-size, brand new bike. I could hardly touch the pedals but that didn't matter, I could ride forever on this machine. At the train station I would meet the other deliverers and the head honcho who would get the bundles of papers off the train and distribute them to us, we would have to fold and roll them and place them in our bags on our bikes.

It was freezing cold on the station platform. If you know Ballarat, the old buildings are made of ironstone, probably built by the convicts and the station is no exception. My fingers would be so cold but I put up with it, my bike was worth it. I would be handed a list of my customers and yes, you guessed it, mine was the hilliest part of Ballarat. I would have to be helped onto the bike as it would topple over every time I tried to get on. When I stopped at any time, I made sure I could hold onto a fence for balance. If I dismounted, which was usually not on purpose, I would just topple over and getting back on was near on impossible. Saturday mornings were the worst. The Age newspaper was massive and I had to make two or three trips. Lucky there was no school on Saturdays. On weekdays I would be running late for school. Dad and I would need to talk. Could I resign? I was no quitter but there was no doubt I was in way over my head.

It didn't take much to talk Dad into it. I had a feeling that he had been talking to my boss. There was a rumour going around that some of the customers didn't like their morning newspaper arriving just in time for lunch. I still had to pay back the money for the bike so the condition was that I had to find my own job. I decided an afternoon job would suit me best, so I started to ask around. The chemist in town was after a smart young man to do odd jobs and I was the man for the job!

My main duty was to ride up to the top of town, to the pharmacy wholesalers, and pick up the orders for the day. Balancing a cardboard box full of pills and medicines on my handlebars was a piece of cake. Just up my alley. I was expected to put in two hours of work from 4.00-6.00 pm and the pay was good. Some nights there were no deliveries so I had to fill in the time cleaning out the back of the shop. How to string the time out was my biggest concern. I loved this job.

The pharmacist was an old guy and sometimes he was just getting back from lunch at the same time I started work. I didn't have much to do with him as I took my orders from the head lady. I soon realised however, that he was drunk as a skunk. He would go to lunch at the hotel where he lived and I doubted if he was ever sober. In those days, chemists mixed a lot of their prescriptions by hand and I'm sure the head lady had done most of the work, she certainly ran the show!

Ballarat was a great place to play and explore. The Eureka Stockade was just up the road from our place. This was steeped in history and our main interest was a giant swimming pool, it had a mud bottom and we would go yabbying in it. Yabbies are a small type of fresh water crayfish. I can remember the day they emptied it by pumping the water out, I think they were going to seal the bottom. We had a bonanza as the sides were riddled with yabby holes and we brought home bucket loads of these delicious little critters.

Near my grandparents house was a place called Black Hill. The large hill was fenced off as it was riddled with mine shafts and old mining equipment. Tonnes of gold had come out of this hill and it was a great place to explore. There were tunnels and caves, as well as old shafts. Some were covered in but none were safe. Naturally it was off bounds to everyone but of course that didn't stop us. There was a walking trail around it and when Mum came with us we stuck to that path but when she wasn't we had a great time.

Our grandparents on Mum's side were called Ninny for our Grandmother and Diddy for our Grandfather, I'm not sure why. I have lots of memories from their house as far back as remembering how we would get from the train station to their house when we were on holidays. It was in a Hansom cab, just like the kind in one of those Sherlock Holmes movies. Milk was delivered by horse and cart with a big milk container and we would go out and collect it in a billycan. An old Chinese guy would deliver fruit and vegies to the door.

Grandparents Diddy and Ninny in Ballarat   At our house in George St. Ballarat

Ninny was a lovely old lady who used to fuss around when we visited as most grannies do and it's easy to see where Mum got her loving nature. Diddy was a different kettle of fish, we were in awe of him, not really scared, but wary of him. He would just sit in his favourite chair and puff on his pipe. He was a retired engineer and wasn't in good health. He had bad eczema, a trait which runs in the family. Graeme suffered a bit from it and I had an Auntie who had it really bad. We weren't too sure how to take him. Glen and I would play in his workshop with all his old tools. He would warn us that this wasn't on, I'm sure he hadn't touched these tools for years but I guess they were sacred to him. In a twist of fate, I was the last person to see him before he died and comfort him.

We lived in Ballarat for about two years then back to Melbourne. Dad liked to change, much like me.

East Preston

On our second visit to Melbourne we found it a much nicer place to live. We had bought a fruit and vegie shop in Plenty Road, East Preston. In those days, Preston was a nice, outer suburban, fast growing little community, nothing like the inner city Carlton. These days it is much the opposite, the Carlton slums have disappeared and being close to the city it is a very trendy place to live. Preston has gone through a change and has become a home for different ethnic groups. This will change again as home values continue to soar.

The war had been over now for nearly five years and Australia's economy was booming. There were plenty of jobs for everyone and the general atmosphere was positive. The gangs of young men roaming the streets of Carlton were non-existent here. Food rationing had ceased. During and after the war a lot of commodities were rationed—food, petrol, some building supplies and lots of other things. Every family was issued with a ration book and no matter how much money you had, you would need a coupon from this book to buy some things. Everything was needed for the war effort, there was a black market of course but most people stuck to the rules. We weren't bothered much by food rationing as we grew our own.

Dad's brothers, Les and Fred, had joined the army. Dad was unable to join with them as he was classed as a primary producer. Farmers, factory managers and other people like this were too valuable at home.

As kids, the war didn't affect us much, we were somewhat sheltered from it, but our parents must have been very concerned as the threat of invasion was very, very real. The Japanese were in New Guinea which was only a stone's throw away from Australia. The Government was downplaying the threat so as not to panic the nation. We heard reports on the radio, but they were mainly positive. Darwin had a few bombs dropped on it, but in reality, the city had almost been destroyed with dozens of ships Australian, American and British sunk in Darwin's harbour. The Japanese, however, made one huge fatal mistake, they bombed Pearl Harbour, which brought America into the war. Without America's help we would've been sitting ducks.

I was to continue my education at Preston Technical College, Glen went to a girl's school in Fitzroy. We were growing up now, Lea was to marry Keith Robertson. They are still married and have brought a lovely family into this world.

I graduated from Preston Tech and Dad said it was time for me to get a job. I had helped out in the shop, going with him on home deliveries and to the Victorian Markets some mornings to buy our stock. This meant getting up at about 4am but it was worth it, very exciting with trucks coming in loaded with vegies and everyone was busy, buying and selling, it was chaotic. I remember coming home one morning when we were involved in a traffic accident, fruit and vegies scattered everywhere across the road. Dad wasn't happy.

Dad asked me "what do you want to be?". I had no idea. "A trade would be best, maybe with the Government, that way you would have security", he suggested, "refrigeration, electrician or maybe a new up and coming thing called electronics." Whatever, it didn't matter much to me. We looked in the paper and the Government Aircraft Factory in Fishermans Bend, Port Melbourne, were looking for apprentices in just about all trades. This sounded good to me, airplanes would be fun.

We made an application. I had good technical qualifications and we were accepted to at least go and check it out anyway. We were shown around the whole factory and I was taken somewhat by the instrument overhaul section. This was a nice, big room, very clean and everyone wore a nice white dust coat. I was to become an Aircraft Instrument Maker.

To get to work I would have to catch a tram into the city, about 40 minutes ride, and walk across the Yarra River, via the Queen Street Bridge and catch a bus to Fishermans Bend, Port Melbourne. In all about 1 ½ hours travel. It didn't matter much in those days, everyone had a job, no dole, you just worked. Some of my friends didn't have such good jobs though, some worked in shops or drove trucks.

I remember my first day. We were interviewed and measured, given ID cards and taken to our respective workplaces. Another kid, Brian Clowes, and I were grouped together, he was to become a lifelong friend.

The usual tricks were played on us by the tradesmen, sent on all sorts of wild goose chase errands but all in all I liked it, especially payday. We soon learned the ropes. The first year of my apprenticeship was spent in the engineering workshop, great basic training. We were to attend schooling at Royal Melbourne Technical College one day a week, this was my fourth technical school. I also did some extra non-compulsory subjects of a night.

We had sold the business and bought a house in Beauchamp Street, East Preston, about three streets from the shop. Dad got a job in the Woollen Mills in Collingwood, it seemed strange for him to have a job working for someone else. He did however, work at the Ford Motor Company factory in Ballarat for a short time before we came back to Melbourne.

Glen was to later get a job in the office at the Woollen Mills, she had previously worked at a pharmacy. Lea had a good job in the office at Wynns Wines, it was in the city I think. We were all going our own way now and it was hard to keep track of everyone. My next big thing was to get myself some wheels. I bought an old Morris convertible and Dad gave me driving lessons. The Morris broke down more times than I can remember and I can recall brother-in-law Keith coming to the rescue on more than one occasion. I decided to fix the car for all time. I pulled it all apart in the backyard. Dad had a feeling that the car was going nowhere and would be in the same spot for years to come. The hints came loud and clear, "quit the Morris and get yourself a real car".

There was a car yard on the next corner and I had my eye on a shiny black Ford. Dad said "don't buy it until we get a mechanic to check it over". What a waste of time, I was going to buy it anyway. It checked out A1, very low mileage and Dad loved Ford V8s. He'd had a few in his time so it was a sale which we all agreed on. I sold the Morris to someone and they had to cart it off in bits and pieces. Dad said that will give them something to do for a while. My car was a 1939 Ford V8, 2 door Sloper, the kind of car you see in old gangster movies. It was 12 years old but in mint condition. It was the envy of everyone and I was very much an Al Capone type character. Girls were even starting to notice me.

Speaking of girls, I wasn't sure what to make of them. I had two sisters but they were like brothers. I hope they don't take that the wrong way but they were different than "real" girls, the ones that I would see with some of my mates. Going to an all-boys school I hadn't had much contact with girls, not since primary school anyway and then they all looked the same, boys and girls I mean. We were going to dances, well I was tagging along with my mates. I must admit, I would have preferred to have been doing something else. It wasn't much fun standing around, although sometimes a girl would ask me to dance, that was fun. Quite often I would walk one home, not too sure how it all came about, it just seemed to happen and at times I wasn't too sure who was walking who home. We would sometimes arrange to meet again the next Saturday night at the same place or maybe somewhere else. I would try and meet them inside as this had certain advantages, for one you didn't have to pay their entry in and two, I don't think you would be really obligated to dance with them all night or even walk them home. You never know a prettier girl may ask me to dance. Now I wasn't being shallow, don't think that, just not sure how this boy/girl thing worked.

When I had my car though, it was all different. It was usually crammed full, most of the time with both boys and girls. There was only one rule, I was to have a girl sitting next to me, this was only fair, being it was my car after all. These teenage years were great. I was playing football, Dad seemed proud of me, although I don't think he was too happy with my social life. My sisters were out of my hair. Lea was getting a bit bossy, she still thought I was a child. The best thing about Glen was that she was bringing home some very hot girlfriends. I was most impressed with a girl named Anne but too scared to make a move. Rejection, so close to home, would've been a disaster. Little did I know until recently, Glen fancied one of my closest mates, Laurie Caldwell. We could've done a deal, Laurie was a big guy who played football with me, a full back. He would look after me on the football field and going out with my sister would've been no trouble whatsoever for him.

Another great memory of these times was the 1956 Olympic Games in Melbourne. I scored some free tickets from work and watched Betty Cuthbert and Shirley Strickland win gold for us. Also, I remember the great Russian long distance runner, Emil Zatopek. TV was first introduced into Australia for these Games. The world was changing rapidly, how rapid I guess we only know now. Computers, social media, it's all happening. We didn't have mobile phones or dozens of other gadgets in those days.

The good thing about this era was no drugs, I certainly wasn't exposed to any. However, I did like a beer after football, the liquor laws were terrible at that time. The pubs closed at 6pm and the "6.00 swill" wasn't pretty. You were allowed to order your drinks up to five minutes to six, then you had to finish them by 6.15pm. Some people would order five or six drinks and down them in 15-20 minutes. The drink drive laws at that time were very lax so how many deaths occurred because of this is unknown. Pubs also closed on Sundays but sly grog dealers were available.

CHAPTER 2

MY SPORTING CAREER

I've always wished my sporting career was as impressive as my love of sports. Warning, this chapter may be boring as it contains lots of self indulgence, self pity, sadness, happiness and just a little euphoria.

I first recognised sport as a good thing early in my life. We all know that it is healthy for your body and also for your general well being, character building and becoming a team player is important. It may also help in developing an ego of giant proportions.

It started in primary school when I was school champ in my age group at running. The whiney little kid could run and to have a blue ribbon gave you respect. Then at Preston Tech they lined us up across the school oval. We had to run the length of the field to see who could run and who couldn't. I blitzed the whole field in a jaw-dropping performance. Yes, the skinny little new kid from the bush could really run. I made the school team in the 100 yard relay at the combined high school games, I then came 10th out of 2,000 in our cross country race which went along the Merri Creek, all the way to Coburg, around Pentridge Gaol and back again. The winner was Ronald Dale Barassi who was in a higher and older group, although I think he was the same age as what I was. He was a legend, even then. Whether he was playing for Melbourne at that time I'm not sure, he was at least playing in the colts. He played for Preston Scouts in the Preston District Junior Football Association, the same Association as my team Regent. I don't recall playing against him though he may have been playing before my time. As I said, he is the same age as me but he might have been playing when he was younger, maybe 12 who knows, he was pretty good.

Another sporting legend of the time was Bill Lawry the cricketer. Bill was a year younger than me and I can remember watching him in our school team. He first made the age team at the school at 12 years of age. He made Northcote's first grade team at 14 and represented Victoria at 17. I was no cricketer but I did get some fame by captaining a team to a premiership in Perth's Mercantile League in later years. We all know where Bill went, he captained Australia and is a great cricket commentator even to this day.

My love of Aussie Rules football started in Carlton when Dad and I would go and watch Collingwood play. My first real participation however, was at Preston. A few of my mates and I attended a registration night at Regent. Regent was like a mini suburb of Preston near Reservoir, it was for the Under 15s at the Regent Football Club. Most of my mates played in the school team, I was on the list but hadn't ever got an actual game in the firsts. When it came to my turn to register the Secretary said "this is for the Under 15s team, the Under 13s is tomorrow night". I said "no, this is where I want to play". He asked me my birth date, 29 December I replied. He said "pity, two more days and you could've played with the little kids" the Coach told me to go and see the Association Secretary to ask if I could play in the lower age grade, "When he sees the size of you, I'm sure he won't mind the two days age difference" he said. This wasn't on, I wanted to play with my mates, after all I'd played with them at school and survived.

The next week I told the coach that the Association Secretary had said "no go, rules are rules, I must play under 15s". I hadn't been anyway near the Association Secretary but I thought a little lie wouldn't hurt. Playing under false pretences wasn't on, it just wasn't right. The coach looked at me and I'm sure under his breath he said "well, it's your funeral". I was lumped with a group of six or seven other players. We were that group that they had to have but didn't really want, the losers, the unco-ordinated, the ones who didn't really want to be there. The Coach, however, had to play us as parent pressure and Association rules demanded it. We would be rotated one by one, each would get a game in turn.

I played a few games without setting the world on fire, however, I made the starting team for the finals. We were to play as a curtain raiser before the last game of the VFL season. It was at Victoria Park, Collingwood's home ground. I had watched football at this venue many times. The game was between Collingwood, who finished on top, and Footscray, who were also a top team. My excitement was unbelievable. Collingwood had all their champions in the team— Bobby Rose, Bill Twomey, Thorold Merrett, Neil Mann. Footscray would have Ted Whitten, he was one of the greatest players of all time. Now it was their turn to watch me play. It is true what they say, players that ran out onto the Melbourne Cricket Ground for a grand final when the crowd roars you could run through a brick wall. This is what they say. Well this was my grand final.

The oval was packed. I guess it was my size, I don't know, maybe my pace. As I ran around the wing in front of the Old Members Stand, the crowd seemed to have adopted me. Every time I went near the ball, they roared, just like they do now with Nick Nat (Nic Naitanui) when he plays for the Eagles. I felt like Superman, I can only remember one passage of play when out one on one with my opponent, all in space on the wing, he went to ground, I hurdled him, yeah, just like Superman, gathered the loose ball and headed for the goals. I thought about having a shot, we needed a goal, but instead I kicked it to our full forward and he kicked the goal. The crowd went wild. If I never played another game I was happy. Unfortunately we lost by two points. At our break up presentation night I received a trophy as one of the Best Players in the Final, also another trophy as Best First Year Player. I had proved myself to the coach who shook my hand and said "well done".

We lost a lot of players next season though, they were too old for our team. Our Captain, Wally Clark, was off to play for Fitzroy in the VFL. He made the firsts immediately. He was a big loss. We also lost our full forward Graham Gotch to Fitzroy. Preston Scouts lost their champ Brian Pert, the father of Gary Pert, himself a Fitzroy legend and present CEO of Collingwood.

I was in for a very big surprise, I was voted Captain. I had my good mate Laurie Caldwell and co-rover Barry Evans playing and maybe they rigged the vote, I'm not sure, but I repaid them though by winning the Best and Fairest Award that year. I also made the combined Association team and we played a team from WA on the Preston Oval. Their team had a player called Ray Gabalech, a man mountain, who the next year played for Collingwood. He was signed up that day by Collingwood. We had our own legend playing for us though, a man called Murray Weederman. He played for an opposition team in our Association and also the next year he played for Collingwood. He was soon made Captain of Collingwood and later coached them. That was the end of my junior football. Next year I had to play against the men.

Regent had an Under 17s team but Barry Evans had signed up with Reservoir, an open age team that played in the Melbourne Metropolitan League. I said "OK, I'll be in that". There were some pretty big kids in under-age football so we were confident we could handle the men. In Aussie Rules, even though it is a contact sport, size doesn't really matter, big or small, there's a position and part you can play. I had realised that the big guys were usually slow so if you kept your wits about you, keeping out of their way wasn't that hard. Also, they were easy to tackle. Race up behind them and tackle around the hips and sit them on their backsides. That soon gained you plenty of respect. I won Reservoir's Best and Fairest that year in a real surprise. We had some very good players so I certainly didn't expect that. I was only barely 16 and still a midget although I was building up a bit in the muscle department.

At the start of next season, I decided to go to a gym and do some weight training. I would call into a gym in the city on my way home from work. Frank Sedgman owned the gym, he was one of the most famous tennis players of all time and lots of other tennis players would train there from time to time. Lew Hoad, Ken Rosewall and I think even the great Rod Laver was sometimes seen.

I remember once, the manager asked me if I was going in a body building competition which was coming up. I wasn't sure what he was on about so he showed me a poster on the noticeboard. I said "are you serious?" "yes, you would be ok in your division" he said. I declined. Not too sure what division I would qualify for. Anyway, I was very fit, especially as I was training two nights a week at Port Melbourne's home ground. This was on my way home, the bus stopped there and it was just down the road a bit from work. Robert Atkinson, known as Acky, was a workmate of mine.

Football mates Me, Greg, Smithy and Skinny Aldridge

He played for Port Melbourne in the VFA as it was known then. He also played for South Melbourne and St Kilda. Little did he know, I was soon to join him at Port Melbourne. He was my mentor when I first arrived at work and neither of us would've guessed that I would play beside him.

I was training by myself at Port Melbourne with the idea of having another season with Reservoir. One afternoon a Port Melbourne official who was watching me running asked me if I would like to train with the Port Melbourne team. "Really, do you think that would be OK?" I said. I had a couple of nights training with them and one night when I got home from work there was a letter from Neil Mann, he was a Collingwood legend who had just retired and was now a Coach. It was an invitation to train with Collingwood. I could hardly believe it. Dad was obviously just as excited but we both kept our emotions in check as us Hunt men do. I said "I think I might give it a bit of thought". Yeah, hardly slept all week, couldn't wait for the next training night. Training with the superstars was like living a dream. All the Collingwood champions were there and I was being introduced to them one by one. Training wasn't that good though. I soon learnt that it was a closed shop. The regular players weren't going to give the recruits a look-in if they could help it.

I played two practice games, the second one I thought was good. I held my own. The next week I was disappointed to find myself in the list of reserves. I guess I didn't show much character and never went back. I wasn't going wait for them to say I wasn't good enough. Dad was no doubt disappointed but he didn't say much. I would go back and play with my mates at Reservoir, at least they would kick the football to me.

After two games with Reservoir, Port Melbourne called and told me I had been selected in the reserves to play Prahan. Prahan were in the VFA in those days. I went well. I remember the game very clearly as I got crunched late in the game. I went into a pack headfirst and was left flattened. A teammate picked me up and I remember his words "son, don't ever do that again if you want to live". My head was spinning but I kept playing. I wasn't going to tell anyone but I no doubt had concussion. In those days, crunching you in the head wasn't a problem it was all part of the game so you never complained. I was soon promoted and played in our finals team on the old St Kilda ground. I was only a reserve but still it was exciting. I was young and we had our strongest team in for the year. I got onto the field for the first time in the last ten minutes. We lost by a few points and we were finished for the year. Little did I know it was my last game for Port.

I had accepted a job at the Naval dockyards in Williamstown. My friend Brian Clowes, from the Government Aircraft Factory

(GAF), and I were both fully fledged tradesmen now. Brian had joined the dockyards, it was closer to his home and he was setting up an instrument workshop there. He asked me to join him and I did. I was waiting to be appointed as an Inspector at work which seemed to take ages, despite being told I had the promotion, nothing was happening. I lacked patience so I jumped ship!

It was a good job but created a problem football wise. There was no Westgate Bridge in those days which meant Port Melbourne and Williamstown were poles apart. No way of getting to training on time. I would have to drive back around and go through the city and then out to Port Melbourne. Training would be over by then and there were no floodlights in those days. Barry Evans had left Reservoir and was playing for Bellfield which was a suburb near Heidelberg, close to Preston, I joined him as it seemed a good option. I knew a lot of the players there but there was one snag, Port refused to clear me. They said I was young and had a future with them. Eventually, they saw reason and agreed I couldn't play if I couldn't train.

In my second season with Bellfield I suffered a severe knee injury. There was no Sports Medicine in those days, just GPs and Medicos at the Club. In today's world I would've had a complete knee reconstruction. Anyway, my football days were over, that was it. I was on the verge of getting married so I thought "too bad, that's life, I'll concentrate on my new family". I did play after nearly two years rest but it was never the same, I had lost my pace. Training was restricted but I did manage a few games playing for Victoria Park in Perth.

In later years, I have had two artificial knee joints, a legacy from playing with injuries. Still, I wouldn't have had it any other way. I enjoyed my footy. I played and coached for some years with Victoria Park and was even President at one stage and am a proud life member of that Club.

While working at GAF, I completed four months national service at Puckapunyal Military Base. I was one of the youngest to be called up. It was the old two day rule again. They gave me the option to defer basic training if I wanted to but I wanted to go. I was 18 on 29

December and four days later I was a soldier. The first month was hard as they whipped us into shape, then it was easier.

I was assigned to the workshops, apparently they thought I was an engineer! Fixing tanks was way out of my reach but it was a cushy job. Another guy, Howe, and I would report for duty and while the others went on route marches and such, we sat in the office doing paperwork which was mainly playing noughts and crosses. I had repaired the Captain's watch so we could do no wrong in his eyes.

We did have to do some training though. I remember one day we had hand grenade throwing drill, it was the real deal with live grenades. We'd had a fair bit of practice throwing dummy ones and it was now time for the real thing. We were in two bunkers with a deep slit trench joining them in the middle. We would be called into the centre one by one, then the Sergeant would hand you a live grenade and you would throw it with a bowling action over the top of the trench which was fairly high at least two metres. The Sarge was to give the orders, one, "ready", two "pull pin", three, "throw". I was next in line and had to observe the procedure while the rest of the platoon stayed in the safety of the bunker.

The Sarge gave the orders and the thrower must've panicked. He pulled the pin and on the order "throw" he either misjudged the height of the trench or just dropped the grenade, I'm not sure, but it just dropped at their feet. The Sergeant dived after it, I was frozen stiff. There was a whole boxful of live grenades, it could've landed in there and I don't like thinking about what could've happened, we could've been blown to kingdom come. Sarge luckily found the grenade in time and threw it out. It exploded with only a few seconds to spare. Sarge, the bad thrower and myself were the only ones who knew what happened that day. We were certainly washing our underwear that night!

Another funny episode happened to me at the rifle range. We would all line up, 20 of us, with 20 targets, two or three hundred metres away. The targets were all numbered. We would have 20 bullets, fire them all at once when the order was given or take your time.

Someone would tally the scores at the target end and relay them back to the officer. I broke the record. Near perfect score.

What really happened was that the guy next to me was inadvertently pumping his shells into my target and with my shots as well I was the "Dead Eye Dick" of the Platoon. He couldn't believe his lousy score which was nil, I knew what was going on but kept my mouth shut! Well wouldn't you? I was young and little and used to hate it when we had drill. I would carry the same weight with all our packs on and as well as that WWI 303 rifle, which I could hardly lift. Some of the big guys, two years older and 6'4" or more carried exactly the same weight. It wasn't fair, so my moment of glory was being the "Bren Gun Champ" of the Platoon. Anyway, who was to say most of the bullseyes weren't mine anyway.

All in all, I think National Service is a good thing and should be on the agenda for today's youth. I know a lot of people see it as training for war, but it's the discipline and teaching respect that's so important. I am anti-war and anti-guns. National Service taught me to respect guns and to handle them safely.

It was about this time that Ninny passed away and Diddy came to live with us. He was very frail and bedridden. His bed was in my room and one morning when I woke up early to go to work, he was out of his bed lying on the floor and talking incoherently. I picked him up and put him back in his bed and he muttered something like "good boy". He seemed a lot more active than normal and I thought no more of it. We had made peace with each other in the few days he was with us, a lot different than the early days in Ballarat when I was a bit wary of him. Anyway, no-one else was up so I went off to work, not arriving back until late. It was a sad house when I arrived home, Mum had got dressed and went in to check on him only minutes after I left. He had passed away.

Anyway, on a brighter note, my love life was just becoming alive. I only had three somewhat serious romances all tolled, the last one ending in marriage. The first one was a girl at work called Elaine. She worked in the office with Brian's girlfriend. She was a nice girl and we hit it off really well. Our first outing was a work social and it was a great night but there was one problem, she lived in Williamstown which meant I would have to make two trips from Preston to Williamstown and back. This was a long way, right across the other side of Melbourne. I was forever travelling backwards and forwards. Some nights I stayed at her place, but I wasn't sure about her Dad. In those days you were a bit wary of the fathers. Her Mum approved and Elaine was happy with that. I took her to either Lea's or Glen's engagement party, I can't remember which it was, but it was in a hall in Preston. Mum liked her and I think she thought "this is a nice girl, a bit different to the ones he normally hangs out with" but it didn't last. It was a lot less trouble and bother hanging out with the Preston girls. My only regret is that I don't think I explained this very well to Elaine and the dockyard office was somewhere to stay well clear of in those next couple of weeks.

My next romance was with a girl called Brenda. She was the girlfriend of one of my best mates, Barry, and very attractive, a part time photographers model. One night at a party, she declared she liked me more than Barry, I was flattered but was worried about Barry, she assured me they were breaking up and I was available so I figured this was OK. I could always bring into play the "all's fair in love and war" rule knowing full well that war could break out at any time but I thought she was worth it. It lasted for about 12 months, she would come to the football and watch me play and we seemed well suited. She loved to party and we attended football socials and some concerts.

Her father died and she asked for some time out. I knew she disliked her father as he was mean to her mother, I'd only met him once but still it was her father and I think I blew it by not being more sympathetic. Neither of us called each other for a while, well ever, I suppose. It was a stand-off. She attended the football games with the other player's girlfriends and even came to the football socials alone. We eyed each other off across the room. My mates were telling me not to worry about her and their girlfriends were telling me to go and talk to her. Anyway, it didn't happen, stupidity on both sides I guess, though more on mine.

Anyway, Gaye was closing in. The little 14 year old who was the sister of one of my mates was growing up. She was a cheeky little thing and now about 15 or 16. I had taken her older sister, Wendy, out a couple of times just to some of those dances where we would meet inside and a few Sunday drives in my new car. Nothing serious, in fact, I knew the whole Penrose family. But everywhere I went I seemed to run into Gaye. I think she had a boyfriend and I remember one day I was outside her place with her brother when a sports car pulled up with her inside. It was a convertible and she had a superior look on her smug little face. I'm not sure what I said to the boyfriend, it wasn't much but I can remember wishing that I'd bitten my tongue. Why would I be even slightly interested in this little pest, was I jealous?

Now Gaye was a feisty proposition. Most of us men are fairly simple creatures and we like to know where we stand when it comes to tangling with the opposite sex. I could tell Gaye was interested in me, flirting when I called in to see her brother but other times ignoring me when I tried to make conversation. Playing games I thought but then again she is a child. Anyway, why should I even bother with her? She was a challenge though and seemed to end up being my girl of choice when I would go to the drive-in movies.

We were married at the Church of England Church in Preston and honeymooned at Marysville. Tragically this guesthouse burnt down in the 2009 Black Saturday bushfires. We moved into my home. Glen and Lea were married and had left home. Lea was living at Keith's family home and Glen bought a house in Blackburn with her husband. Mum made Gaye welcome but I'm not sure Dad knew what to make of her. They both had strong personalities. Gaye was no submissive little wife I can tell you that.

Just got married at Preston on the 3rd of December, 1960

Outside the Church

A bit later we were expecting a baby and thought it was time to find our own house. Accommodation was tight, we didn't have the money to buy and rentals were scarce. I had always wanted to travel and thought this would be impossible once we were settled as a family. I applied for jobs interstate and was accepted fairly quickly in both Tasmania and Western Australia. The West Australian job appealed to me more, it was with an airline. They would pay all expenses for us to relocate in Perth, I would drive my car and Gaye would follow later by air. Gaye wasn't happy and at first refused to go. She was from a large family and the bond with her siblings was strong. I knew we were doing the right thing though, it was time for me to leave the nest and take control. Gaye came around. I promised her we could always come back if it didn't work out.

Dad was worried, it was no piece of cake driving to Perth. The Nullarbor Plain was over a thousand miles of unmade road and in places just a track. It wasn't a trip many people had made. He said I shouldn't do it alone and advertised in the paper for a travelling companion. This was pretty normal back then. A woman answered the advertisement and we went to interview her. She was middle-aged, a good driver and very sensible. Dad loved her. I took an instant dislike to her, she would take control and I could see myself abandoning her in the middle of the Nullarbor, that's if she made it that far. The Gods were with me however, and she backed out at the last minute. It was nothing to do with my prayers, some family problem apparently.

I set off one Saturday morning in my car, a fairly new Holden. The car was packed with all my wordly possessions. Dad and Mum were fussing around, Dad giving me all sorts of advice. He had given me his rifle which was a big deal and I accepted it with glee. There was no sign of Gaye, was she inside crying because she would miss me or just sulking? She did come out eventually and wished me luck. She would stay for two or three months until I got settled, then she would join me. I wasn't sure how she would get along with Dad during this time though but that's another story.

CHAPTER 3

THE BIG TRIP

I guessed that the trip would take me about a week and the first day was plain sailing. I reached Adelaide and camped by the side of the road about 100 kms from the city. The next day the car was overheating and I had to top up the radiator quite a few times from roadside puddles. I limped into Crystal Brook which was the next town. The garage guy said that it was a core plug and he would have to drop the gearbox. It would take a couple of hours. Repairs didn't cost all that much it was just mainly labour.

On my way again and cruising along on the last bit of bitumen before the dreaded Nullarbor Plain. It was rough going on the Nullarbor Plain sliding all over the road in places as it was very sandy. Camping out of a night was surreal, so quiet and I'd hardly seen another car or person. At night, the whole place came alive with pairs of eyes shining in the headlights, wombats, foxes, dingoes, lizards, the whole countryside was jumping. During the day they just all disappeared. My car radio could pick up Queensland, thousands of miles away. In those days, car radios were a fairly new invention and reception was generally quite poor. Fuel could've been a problem if you misjudged your economy. These days the Eyre Highway is a major road with quite a few motels and roadhouses but back then there was only three fuel outlets for the whole thousand miles. One of these outlets was just a single bowser by the side of the road and you were in luck if the attendant was on duty. If not, you just waited until he turned up.

On a bad stretch of track, I had two punctures but luckily I had two spare tyres. When I reached Eucla which was just a roadhouse, the guy on duty said that he had been waiting for me and that he could fix my punctures. I'm not sure how he knew I had tyres to mend as I hadn't seen anyone else on the track that day! Bush telegraph I thought.

I was now in WA and glad to get to Norseman. Bitumen at last, love that smooth black stuff! Into Kalgoorlie and shouted myself a cooked meal and then back on the road. The Holden came to a shuddering halt about 100 miles out of Kalgoorlie, the next town was Southern Cross, more than a 100 miles away. I was stuck in the middle of nowhere! A passing motorist stopped and said he knew the mechanic in Southern Cross and would ask him to come to my rescue. I couldn't leave the car as it was fully loaded with all my goods. So I sat and waited, hours went by, no more traffic on the road and it was getting dark. Then headlights appeared on the horizon, it was the garage guy from Southern Cross! He told me that I was very lucky as he had been told that I was just out of Southern Cross a few miles. He had just about given up finding me and was about to turn around when he saw me.

He had a quick look at the car and said that I'd done a timing gear and needed to be towed into town. He had a Holden, just like mine. He attached a tow-rope and off we went. He told me not to turn my headlights on as it would dazzle him. We started off fairly steadily but he gradually increased his speed until we were doing nearly 60 miles an hour which was over 100 kms an hour. I had to focus hard as it was pitch black and dead scared I was going to run into him as the tow-rope was less than 10 metres long. I was hanging on for grim death and it seemed like we would never make it.

We eventually pulled into his garage and he had one of his workers help push me into the workshop. He said "you are some driver, I hardly felt you. I had to check a few times to see if you were still there". I was in shock, I stepped out of the car and it was like someone setting foot on dry land after being lost at sea. I could've kissed the ground I'm sure.

They started work on it right away as the parts needed to be ordered before 10 pm for delivery in the morning. It was already after 8.00 pm and it was closing time. The mechanic wanted to knock-off I'm sure but they got stuck into it. He wanted to take me to the pub to get a room but I knew I didn't have the money to spend on hotel accommodation and God only knows how much the car repairs and towing was going to cost. I only had enough cash for fuel. No credit cards in those days. I wanted to sleep in the car but he insisted and bundled me into his car and off to the pub. He said to the manager "Look after my friend. He needs a bed and by the look of him he needs a good feed as well". I mentioned to my new friend that I was concerned about the cost of all this and told me to worry about that tomorrow. I thought "in for a penny in for a pound". An old saying I suppose but yes, I was so hungry and tired I WILL worry about it tomorrow.

I had a steak, well why not? Money was of no object, I think I was delirious. I had a shower and slept like a log. I sat up in the bed the next morning and reality had set in. I would be stuck in this town for some days. I had left some money with Gaye and told her to send it to me if I got stuck. She was still working at her job at the pharmacy so she would have money and my parents would help, but time was of the essence. I had to start work in a couple of days and a bank transfer could take that long.

I considered robbing a bank, after all how hard could it be? I still had Dad's rifle hidden away in the boot of the car. First I had to get out of the pub, I could just pretend I had amnesia when it came to paying the bill. I walked down the stairs looking for the back door but all I found was the manager. He said "just in time for breakfast", I told him I wasn't hungry and just asked for the bill, he hummed and hahed and said, "10 bob should cover it". 10 shillings? The steak alone cost more than that!! No doubt my garage friend had told him to take it easy on me. I paid him and he said "now, about that breakfast, you'd better hurry before the cook packs up".

I walked to the garage, it was only a couple of blocks away and was just in time to see them finish the repairs. The owner took it for a test run and pulled up at the petrol pump and filled the tank, "well, why not" I thought. I thanked him for all his trouble and asked how much I owed him, he went into the office and had a chat with the cashier. I stood there wondering if he would take my golf clubs as payment, they were near new and very expensive. I had nothing else except a lot of junk and Dad's rifle. Did they play golf in this town? I hoped so. He came out of the office and stuffed a piece of paper in my top pocket and told me I could fix him up when I started my new job. Was it my birthday? Was it Christmas? I could've kissed him!

I drove out of town on a high and it wasn't until after lunch, some 200 miles down the track that I was game enough to take the bill out of my pocket to see how much it was, I forget exactly what the amount was as it was in pounds in those days. I think it was around £35. I worked it out in my head. That would only cover parts, petrol and some of the labour. Towing for 100 miles and coming out to find me would cost a fortune. I sent him a cheque and thanked him. He sent a receipt back with a little note at the bottom that read "I'm an excellent judge of character". This experience of human nature stood me in good stead for the rest of my life. I hoped I could live up to this standard.

The rest of the trip was a piece of cake, the car was running perfectly and coming through the hills out of Perth, I wondered where the desert was that they speak of in Melbourne. Heading down Greenmount Hill it was just on dusk and the lights of the city were beautiful. It was like coming to the Promised Land, I'm sure I'm going to love this city.

I drove into the city to have a look. I didn't let a little thing like driving down the wrong way in Hay Street worry me. After all, they needed to update their signs. All the cars tooting me didn't bother me either. "What a welcome" I thought, "they know I'm a Victorian by my number plates and they love me!". I drove back out to Guildford, I would make this my base as it was near the airport where my job was. I found a park and camped the night. When I woke I found I was in the Guildford cemetery, no problems, at least I slept well. I needed accommodation and thought guesthouses would be the way to go. I bought a paper and found someone who wanted a boarder. It was in Midland, not far away so I went to check it out. Little did I know, this family would become lifelong friends and they would have a major impact on me for the rest of my life.

Mrs Hodder was the landlady and she has only just passed away this year, well into her nineties. I placed a piece in the death notices to the effect that she was everybody's Mum and she certainly was to me in those first few weeks. I don't know whether it was luck or what, but the first people I had made contact with in WA were real gems.

Mrs Hodder had a son, also named Charlie, the same age as me with similar interests, a younger brother Brian and a sister called Betty who was a trainee nurse. Charlie had a girlfriend called Wendy, she was interested in Gaye and was looking forward to meeting her. The Hodders played baseball and Charlie was a star player with the Swans, who were the top side in the baseball competition. I went on Sundays to watch and on Saturdays we went to the football. Betty was learning to play squash and as I had played a fair bit of this, she and I played a couple of nights a week. I was like another son to this family and they seemed to like showing me off to their friends. I was a Victorian and in those days a bit of a rarity over in Western Australia.

Gaye was arriving and we needed a place of our own. One of Charlie's baseball friends was moving into their new house and their flat was available, it was in Bassendean, not far away so I grabbed it. Betty came along to help me get it shipshape. Gaye arrived and a big fuss was made of her. She was heavily pregnant. My mother and father came over from Melbourne to stay for Christmas and on Christmas Eve little baby Lisa arrived. A Christmas miracle.

Dad and Mum arrive at Perth Airport for their first visit

Gaye with best friend Wendy

CHAPTER 4

EARNING A LIVING

I started work with MacRobertson Miller Airlines (MMA as it was called) or better known as Mickey Mouse Airlines. My new job was going well, the work was familiar and I could handle it easily. It was the overhaul of aircraft instruments, mainly navigational. I was encouraged to do some courses with the Department of Civil Aviation (DCA), this would allow me to work on aircraft. Also, MMA would send me to do a course on automatic pilot servicing and testing and also later on an electronics course. We had about a dozen technicians working in the overhaul workshop and I was promoted to Leading Hand after our foreman unexpectedly resigned. I was given the job of testing and certifying the autopilots on the F28 Fokker airplanes. After all, I was the expert and had a certificate from DCA to prove this.

This had never been done before by MMA staff. Previously they would have to send the airplanes east or Qantas would have to fly an expert West to do the job. I would save the company thousands of dollars if I could handle the job. "No worries", I thought, I had a black box, controller and a manual with all the procedures listed in it. We would fly down the coast to Bunbury and back again. Once in the air and clear of the metropolitan area, the pilot handed over the controls to me. I was in charge. I programmed the first test and pushed the button, the aircraft did a sudden roll and almost flipped on its back. It was meant to do this but it was a lot more sensitive than I thought. We were on the verge of flying upside down. I matched the astonished looks on the pilot's faces with a look of my own. My look said "Well, this is an important manoeuvre and the aircraft had passed it OK so we all should be looking happy!". I nodded to the speechless pilots and thought, "Just get over it, after all there are no passengers on board, we won't be sued and we're still alive aren't we?" Once I got the hang of it the rest of the tests went according to the manual. I was to test plenty of other autopilots without anymore incidents. I never came across those two pilots in any of the other tests though. Strange, I guess they didn't like flying upside down.

Another good job was calibrating compasses on helicopters. We would go out into the grassed section of the airport between the runways and an apprentice would mark out the main co-ordinates with his master compass and I would sit in the chopper with the pilot and adjust the compass accordingly. We would fly up about 20 metres and the pilots would line up the chopper with the co-ordinates. Afterwards we would do a test flight, usually over the city. We were now testing and overhauling instruments for charter companies and needed more staff. We shifted into a big new workshop and recruited more staff, mainly from overseas. I was now second in charge with a lot more responsibilities.

However, in the airline business nothing stands still. Ansett airlines made a takeover bid for MMA. We were the only commercial airline allowed to fly in WA. Ansett and TAA were the domestic carriers for the rest of Australia and Qantas flew exclusively on overseas routes. Ansett would be sending their instruments over east to Melbourne, to their main workshop so they would close down our outfit. Most of MMAs staff were to be made redundant, they would only need engineers with aircraft licences and would work on what they called line maintenance.

When aircraft fly into Perth, they must be serviced and turned around to fly onto their next destination. Refuelling and catering weren't the only jobs, the aircraft would have to be checked for airworthiness and any faults rectified. I had both DCA instrument and electrical licences so my job was safe. However, I wasn't keen on my new duties. It would involve shiftwork and I had a feeling I would be relocated to Sydney or Melbourne eventually. Line maintenance also was a very stressful job, the aircraft would have to be made airworthy on time to keep up to the airline's schedule. Delay a departure and the company wasn't happy, I can tell you. The pilot's might just decide their flying hours were up and a new crew would have to be brought in. On the other hand, you would have to submit the paperwork to DCA with your signature on the bottom. Most times you wouldn't do the work yourself, you would just supervise so if there was an incident, your neck was on the line and the worst case scenario was being charged for manslaughter if you had a crash.

I had my own little business at home, repairing watches and clocks of a night. I had made friends with some of the jewellers in Perth repairing watches for them on a subcontracting basis. One shop in the Melville Shopping Centre was owned by Ron Brown and he wanted to retire. He asked me if I would be interested in buying the shop. He told me "it is a good little business and I don't want all that much for it". With my redundancy package from MMA and if we sold our house, I would have enough money to buy it outright, no bank finance would be needed.

I resigned from MMA but it wasn't that easy, it never is!! The General Manager called me into his office and said "I don't want to accept your resignation, you are a required employee", he also added, "if you resign, you aren't entitled to any of the redundancy packages, this is only for the ones we put off ourselves. Think about that." I thought about it. Surely he wouldn't do that to me, we were friends. I said "sorry Mr Butcher my mind is made up, I am fully committed to my next venture, I will just have to take what you give me". I was shattered though, we would have to sell the house almost immediately otherwise we were sunk. He smiled and said "It was worth a try.", shook my hand and said "Goodluck, we will give you the full package which includes our superannuation contributions.".

I was to become a business proprietor and a jeweller but I'm getting ahead of myself, we needed to go back to Bassendean and the little flat which now housed three of us including baby Lisa.

CHAPTER 5

OUR FIRST HOUSE

The little flat we had was at the back of the main landlord's house and even though Lisa was a very good baby she did cry sometimes so we decided it was time to find our own home. A bit further down the road there was a new housing estate, it was at Dianella and houses seemed to be a lot more affordable than Melbourne. We could move in by selling my car and my golf clubs as this would give us the required deposit. I think the total price of the house was £4,500. It doesn't sound like much but my weekly wage was only about £25 and this was quite good in those times.

The house was very basic but it was solid brick and had a tiled roof. We were impressed. There was no floor coverings, no window treatments, hardly any kitchen cupboards but it had an electric stove. The flat had a wood stove and to do the laundry we had to boil up a copper so this was like a luxury. We had no furniture, only a bassinette and pram for Lisa, no car but plenty of enthusiasm.

Wendy had taken Gaye under her wing and they had bonded, to this day they are still best friends. They have both survived many ups and downs over the next 50 years. Wendy suggested we look at buying some furniture at the auctions, there was one of those second hand auction houses near her work and her boss knew the manager. She got a bargain, we furnished the whole house for around £20. The furniture wasn't modern, just old fashioned solid Jarrah. We had a bedroom suite, a dining room suite and a few other bits and pieces, enough to get by. We hung some old sheets for privacy on the windows and would take out the back seat of our car and use it as a couch when we had visitors.

I had bought a little Austin A40 for a bargain price. It turned out to be a great little car. I can remember we travelled down to Albany on one occasion when Lea and Keith came over to visit us. The car never missed a beat but Keith suffered a bad asthma attack.

I got stuck into the garden. The front yard was just a plowed paddock but I planted a lawn which grew very quickly. The back yard was a jungle which took some clearing. A man would come around every Sunday selling plants and small shrubs, we would buy one every week, only one, that's all we could afford. We soon had a nice hibiscus hedge running down the driveway.

Our next door neighbours were a young couple who soon became our friends. John and Elma Thompson and they had a boy Ian the same age as Lisa. John was a school teacher who later on went on to become one of WA's top educators and sadly passed away this year.

Showing off our new family at our first trip back home.
Taken at our old Beauchamp St house

We now had a new addition to the family, a boy Graeme. Gaye had a far better time with this birth. She had a difficult time with her first pregnancy, spending a fair bit of time in Swan Districts Hospital.

Wendy and Charlie were now married and later she was to give birth to a girl Leanne. We got to know Leanne very well as Gaye would mind her when Wendy was working full time. Leanne has grown into a lovely young woman and is now of WA's top speech therapists.

We travelled back to Melbourne on holidays to show off our new family and MMA provided the airfares.

I was now playing football again. One of my workmates was Harry Outridge and he coached the Victoria Park Football Team. First I tried out with the Perth Football Club in the WAFL. I trained for a couple of weeks but had trouble with my residential qualifications. This put a stop to my career with Perth. I was bound to Swan Districts as I had lived in Midland and Bassendean. I couldn't get to training with Swans as this was pre-Austin days and I had no transport. I settled for playing with Vic Park but my knee was playing up so I was restricted to playing only a few games. However, I continued on in the administration side of the Club, coaching them for two years and even had a term as President. I am a proud life member of the Club. I have made lots of friends through this Club, Matt Wood being probably the closest.

CHAPTER 6

SECOND HOUSE

Things were going well at work and at home and it was time to update our accommodation. We discovered a lovely house for sale only a few streets away in Jacobsons Way, Morley. It was a lovely cream brick house far superior to our Lennard Street home which would be classified these days as a "first home buyer's dream". This had all the mod cons including luxurious carpets, a lock-up garage, an electric storage hot water system, nothing like the little instantaneous electric heater in the other house. It had a fourth bedroom or study which I could use as a workshop for my watch and clock repairs.

The kitchen, you should've seen it! Wall to wall cupboards with drawers that opened and closed at a touch! I had a go at building some cupboards in the Dianella house and carpentry not being my strong suit, it didn't go all that well. I had never worked in Jarrah before and this strange redwood was almost impossible to saw or screw or nail. A friend said to me "why didn't you use pine?" Now you tell me! I can remember one drawer, Gaye had to get me to open as it kept getting stuck while another one wobbled about and sometimes it would just pull right out spilling knives and forks all over the floor. Gaye would spit the dummy which wasn't unusual.

The kitchen never was a place that had good karma. On our first morning in Dianella at breakfast time, Gaye asked me what I wanted for breakfast. "How about some eggs on toast?" I replied. She said, "I can do the toast but not too sure about the eggs". You're right, she had no idea how to cook. I also had no idea that she was clueless in this department. We had lived at my parents place when first married and I'd always cooked my own breakfast as I would be first up of a morning and on my way to work before the rest of the family were awake. Her speciality was tea and toast, in fact, it was the only thing she could cook. Needless to say there was quite a bit of tension in the kitchen at times.

One of the features of this great house was that it was right next to a lovely park and we had a gate in the backyard which opened out onto this park. Lisa and Graeme would play there and we could keep an eye on them. I remember helping them to make kites and running around in the park flying them. Also, this house came complete with chooks. A lovely enclosure, covered with a shady passionfruit vine was their home. Fresh eggs and passionfruit all in one. Another feature of this house was enclosed eaves in the roof. The house in Dianella had open eaves and a family of pigeons had moved in. Not being too sure how to get rid of them, it was a problem. They would coo and cluck all night and they were starting to stain the ceilings. I didn't want to poison them and I was in desperate need of a pigeon whisperer to try and tell them to bugger off and find somewhere else to live. So we would have no problem with pigeons in Morley, even if they followed us, they wouldn't be able to get into the ceiling. We had this covered.

So, we moved in and Lisa went to primary school at Morley Park Primary School and Graeme to Kindergarten. Unfortunately we didn't spend a lengthy period of time in this house as we had bought the shop which was situated in the suburb of Melville, this was south of the river near Fremantle. We would have to relocate to be closer to the business. The house sold almost immediately, which wasn't a surprise and we moved into a house in Norma Road, Alfred Cove.

CHAPTER 7

MY WIFE

The best part of writing an autobiography is that you can put your own point of view forward with no fear of contradiction. I'm sure if Gaye was writing this she would paint me as the difficult one. She would be wrong of course! We've had our ups and downs as all marriages have, with two major separations, the second one coming after she was in remission from lung cancer. She is very lucky to be alive as when she was diagnosed, survival rates of this disease was less than 2% and she was only in her 30s.

She has endured a lot and is very tough and these days she is a bit fragile with the chemo treatment affecting her somewhat. She has lost her hearing and this had a major impact on our relationship. We are now separated again, for the third time. However, we just live around the corner from each other and remain good friends. We have been married for 52 years and have known each other for nearly 60 years so there is a strong bond. Our marriage has produced two beautiful children and two lovely grandsons and I thank her for that. Now for the real Gaye . . .

I first met her when she was about 14, I had seen her before as I was a friend of her family and I've covered this previously. One evening I was sitting in my car with my girlfriend Brenda, outside her house just around the corner from Gaye's house. We had just pulled up and were about to go into a party when there was a tap on my window. It was Gaye and she handed me a bottle of champagne. I said "What's going on? What's this for?". Nearly said, "Who the hell are you?". She said, "I've just come from my sister Patty's wedding and I have this champagne for you". I was puzzled and said "Thanks but what's it all about?". She said in a sarcastic manner "Well, I'm too young to drink, I'm only a child you know." The message was I suppose "Take some notice of me.". I didn't get that message at the time though. I said to Brenda "Lets give the party a miss and go somewhere and drink the champers". We would have our own little party. Brenda asked "Who was that strange little girl?"

Gaye has learned to cook but still finds it a bit challenging. Her favourite dish is Apricot Chicken which she cooks 2-3 times a week. She reads the directions step by step from the recipe even now, though she must've racked up a few Apricot Chickens by now. Another favourite is her orange cake. Every time we would have guests they would get Orange Cake. Also direct out of the recipe book, absolutely authentic, step by step. When we were first married I could always tell what day of the week it was by the evening meal. Sausages and salad Monday night, stir fry Tuesday night, fish and salad Friday night and so on and sausages and salad again on Saturday lunch and usually takeaway for dinner. However, her Christmas puddings are legendary and son-in-law Paul and our grandsons, Will and Pete being her major fans. She makes the pudding with top of the range organic ingredients also to a special recipe.

We've had some great times. An Asian holiday with good friends Judy and Phil was fantastic. A New Zealand holiday with Graeme was also great. However, I am the envy of all married men in Augusta, living my own life, doing what I want, when I want, when I like. I can do my housework when I feel like it, I can leave my jacket on the chair for days without hanging it up, I can leave my newspaper on the table without folding it up and putting it away, I can watch cricket and football if I wish and in fact I could watch TV all day if it suits me.

Gaye's housekeeping is also legendary, with her favourite weapons being her feather duster and vacuum cleaner. She would drive me crazy and I can remember as far back to our first little house in Dianella. No vacuum cleaner, just a deadly broom. Swishing it around under my feet at breakfast time. Once morning I complained "can't you just leave it for a few minutes until I leave for work?". I copped a face full of butter which was the nearest weapon she could get her hands on. I responded with "the joke's on you, now you have to wash my shirt". Later on I thought I was just playing into her hands as another favourite of hers was doing the laundry, she's in love with her washing machine.

I still check on Gaye each day, doing odd jobs and doing her shopping if need be. I also cook some meals for her as she sometimes goes on a diet of ice-cream and chocolate. If you spoke to her, she would say I don't spend enough time with her, especially when she wants to go shopping. Shopping with her is torture. I am not the most patient man in the world and I realise this.

Anyway, I don't know what brought this on, we were going to open our shop in Melville Shopping Centre so we'd better get back to that.

Lisa Congratulating Gaye on her 70th birthday

CHAPTER 8

MELVILLE JEWELLERS

We took over the business on Saturday morning. In those days, the only weekend shopping was on a Saturday morning from 9-12 and it was generally chaotic as everyone scrambled to do their week's shopping in those three hours. I had recruited a skilled tradesman who had been retrenched from MMA, Tom Clarke, who would become a great friend and loyal employee. He was a very good watchmaker as well.

I also needed a salesgirl as Gaye could only work part-time, Lisa had started school at Booragoon Primary School but Graeme still needed supervision. A young girl named Margaret Legina applied for the job, she lived locally and seemed suited for the position. Ian and Peta Smart said they would lend support. Ian was the coach of Vic Park Football Team and he and his wife Peta were good friends. Ian was very enthusiastic but a bit of a worry, I had to watch him as he would give customers all sorts of advice on their jewellery. He meant well I suppose.

We survived the morning and for the next few years the business thrived. Tom and I would handle the watch and clock side of things and we had a very good jeweller who had his own business but was handling our jewellery on a contract basis, Alan Linney was the previous owner's apprentice and was now a fully fledged tradesman. How lucky we were to get him to do our work. Alan is now recognised internationally as a great jeweller. He had a workshop in London Court and later at the Pioneer Village in Armadale. Gaye worked for him for a while in the Village after we had sold our businesses. Alan is certainly

WA's best known jeweller, with shops in Subiaco, Broome and some leading hotels. His work with Broome Pearls and Argyle Diamonds is world acclaimed.

Two other young girls were employed at this time and were real gems. Angela was a sweetie and Annette Stanley would become a lifelong friend, as would Margaret of course.

I soon became aware of the pitfalls of owning a jewellery business. The burglar alarm was very sensitive and I would get phone calls from the police at all hours of the night. Even a moth could set the alarm off and as the police station was just across the road in Canning Highway they would call telling me to turn the alarm off. They wouldn't say whether we had had a break in or not so I'd rush to the shop only to find it was a false alarm. However, we did have one burglary. The thieves bypassed the alarm by chipping a hole in the shop window and hooking out watches and jewellery. The stupid alarm didn't go off this time. That's the way it goes I suppose and of course, the insurance company didn't pay up, nothing in the policy to say you were covered for this sort of robbery. Typical. The worst part of this was that I would have nightmares. Hearing alarm bells and waking up in the middle of the night not sure if I was dreaming or not. I would wake Gaye up and say "Did you hear that?". She would just look at me say say "Idiot, what's wrong with you?". Maybe she was right, I was losing it!

I was the newly elected President of the Traders Association and the Centre Manager asked if I'd like to go on a fact finding mission to check out shopping centres over east. Down the road a bit in Booragoon they were building a massive shopping centre, the biggest in Perth. This would have a major detrimental effect on our smaller Centre. We had to draw up a strategy to combat this. A plan of attack. We first visited a shopping centre in Brisbane, it was the sister centre to the new one being built in Booragoon. It was also called Garden City. I was impressed. Then we visited three or four centres in Sydney and in Melbourne. The shop was in good hands while I was away. Tom was in charge, along with Gaye. Margaret was very capable and was growing into a lovely young woman. She was to marry Mike Woodward and they would become great friends of ours with many good times spent together. Annette was to marry John Walker and we went to their wedding and met her sisters Robyn and Jenny. They would both work for us in years to come. It always seemed we had a Stanley girl on the payroll at most times. They too, were to become a great asset. We had also attended Margaret and Mike's wedding and we are priviledged to be close friends with her lovely family.

Tom is very special, he is now well into his eighties and has lost his sight. His first wife passed away when he was into his sixties. He then met and married his childhood sweetheart, Betty. A true love story and he deserves his happiness.

CHAPTER 9

GARDEN CITY SHOPPING CENTRE

On arriving back from over east on our fact finding trip a letter was waiting for me from the Garden City letting agents. They wanted me to contact them urgently. They would offer me a shop in their new Centre. It would have a prime location right near the main entrance and it was also facing onto the entertainment area. Only one snag though, they needed an answer right now. One of Perth's leading jewellers had signed up for this shop but he was now too ill to continue. The Centre was to open in a few weeks with most shops ready to go. "Where do I sign?" I asked. I had visited the Brisbane Garden City and it was first class. Every day it was packed with shoppers.

I was confident that I had a good product, my business was built on service and the only other jeweller that was in Garden City was a franchise jewellers who only employed salespeople. I could do a lot better than that. I couldn't wait to get home to tell Gaye. I suppose I should've discussed it with her first but the decision had to be made there and then. She would understand. I'd seen that look on her face before, it meant "Idiot!". She said, "Let's get this straight, we now have two shops?", "Yes, yes" I said "isn't it great? We will sell Melville of course so all will be fine and dandy". We would make the shop an exclusive jewellers, not like Melville which was more of a gift shop. I went to bed but could hardly sleep, making all sorts of plans. I would first resign as President of the Melville Traders Association, I was now in the enemy camp and it would be a conflict of interest.

Barry Urquhart, the Centre Manager wasn't impressed. He said "I guess your shop is now on the market?". "Yes, I said", "Did you realise you have less than six months left on your lease? Who will buy a business with only six months left on the lease?" he asked. "But you just offered me a lengthy extension" I said. "Yes, but that was you. I don't know the person who you might come up with as a prospective buyer and also the Commonwealth Bank has their eye on your shop. They are next door to you and want to expand." I was all pumped up and very positive. Minor detail I thought and put the shop in the hands of a broker.

I took Gaye to Garden City to look at the new shop, it was certainly a great location. She said "This is it? Two walls and a ceiling? That's all there is to it?" "You have to use your imagination" I said "It will be fantastic!". "Yeah and what are we going to use for money to build this fantastic shop?" she asked. I had thought of that but still hadn't come up with an answer. I'm not sure who said it, I think it was a famous comedian but Gaye was now repeating it over and over "Nice pickle you've got us into now Charlie boy".

The next day I was sitting on a box in the middle of the two walls and a ceiling shop, pad in hands scribbling down all sorts of notes. Then I would measure with a tape and step it all out. I had firm thoughts of what I wanted but no idea how to go about it. I was approached by a young man who introduced himself, he was a designer, an architect, a shop designer, whatever, I wasn't really listening. He showed me his portfolio of his designs. No-one had taken him up on any of them so far but if I was interested he would do a design for me and he already had some ideas. He'd obviously been eyeing off the shop. He even had some sketches there and then. He was doing some sort of Masters Degree at Uni. I'm not sure. I wasn't really all that interested. He said "I will do it all for free of course as it will be part of my course. I will price it out and supervise the construction". Did I hear "FREE"? I was certainly listening now. He showed me a design. Solid brick construction, rendered and painted cream. It had long, narrow display windows as he explained the corner location with two big plate glass windows would be very expensive and also no good for security. He suggested a chocolate coloured carpet with jarrah counters and showcases. He even had a design for the external sign. It would be simply cut out of plywood and painted chocolate. "Very inexpensive and far classier than bright neon signs" he said. I hired him, there and then, he was my man.

I then approached a man who appeared to be in charge of the fitting out of a nearby shop. He was interested in building my shop as he had nearly finished all his other shop in the Centre. He was also a local guy and I liked that. I was straight off to my bank. They were to have a branch in the Centre and I had learnt that when a new branch opens the manager has heaps of cash to spread around to attract new customers. I had got him at precisely the right time. He would bankroll the building of the shop, well after all as he said "you have a great little shop in Melville for sale" and he was certainly impressed. I didn't tell him that the "great little shop in Melville" was unsellable though. I did tell Gaye however, that I had thought of a great name for the business—Charles Gaye Jewellers!

Two gorgeous kids

Lisa and Graeme with cousins Gavin and Tracey

CHAPTER 10

CHARLES GAYE JEWELLERS PART A

The shop fitters were doing well. The shop was taking shape. I gave the Manager an advance payment as an incentive to finish the job on time. I didn't want to be paying rent on a half finished shop. The new display cabinets had arrived from the cabinet makers and the chocolate carpet was laid. We were all excited and getting ready to open. One thing was missing though. I had nothing to sell. I could take stock from Melville but this just wasn't the type of jewellery I wanted to sell.

The jewellery wholesalers and manufacturers were queuing up eager to get their goods into this flash new shop. I sounded them out and as my credit was good they would give me plenty of time to pay understanding that it would take me time to get established. I crossed my heart and said "hope to die if I renege on payment" adding under my breath "hope you guys are all very patient". I was to become the local agent for Longines and Citizen watches. I was a friend of Bill Reed who was the proprietor of Broome Pearls so he would give me a nice range of his pearls. Bill was later to hook up with Alan Linney and have a very successful partnership in Alan's shops. I was on a roll.

The business broker had come up with a buyer for Melville, a local lady who made her own jewellery who was very interested. She apparently wanted to buy the business some years ago but I had got in first. There was no hassle with the lease so I guess she had done a deal with the Centre Management, there was also no quibbling with the price, she wasn't going to miss out this time! I paid the bank back and was on cloud nine. She didn't want the workshop at Melville and this suited me. I had new workbenches made for Tom and a jeweller but it meant that I didn't have to buy new special equipment and tools as we had these at Melville. I even had a nice little office for myself and the giant safe, which was nearly big enough to be a walk-in type arrangement. I guess in reality it was the size of a large refridgerator.

Margaret and Annette were to come along with Tom of course. Gaye would be able to work full time as Graeme had joined Lisa at Booragoon Primary. We had hired a suitable housekeeper/cleaning lady called Mrs Starr. Gaye would have more important duties in the business so this would free her up. Mrs Starr was about the tenth cleaner that had tried out for the job. Gaye was a hard task master when it came to cleaning, also she would clean the house herself in the morning before the cleaner arrived for duty. I could never understand this. Also Mrs Starr fitted the suitable age bracket that Gaye liked. No young ones, they are useless she said. Also, Mrs Starr would keep me in check. The young ones will twist you around their little finger was Gaye's reasoning. I don't know about that.

The girls had worked out a nice uniform for the shop. It was a creamy mustard colour which went well with the chocolate carpet. I loved that carpet but the girls hated it. Every little bit of fluff showed up so they were forever vacuuming. The opening of the Centre was spectacular, lots of entertainment, publicity and lots of people. I even bought a new suit and looked the part. I had to get used to customers calling me Mr Gaye. Once of the pitfalls of the name I guess. But the shop was going gangbusters and I had plowed most of the money back into the business. Paying off the stock and investing in new and classier jewellery. However, we did allow ourselves some of the spoils. Gaye bought herself a new canary yellow Toyota Celica and I got rid of my old Holden stationwagon and traded it in on a new GT Falcon muscle car. My first ever brand new car and I soon racked up my first speeding ticket.

We also bought ourselves a house. It was in Stirk Road, Alfred Cove. Not far from the shop. We had been in three rental properties since we had sold our Morley home and the security of owning your own home was a great feeling. It was a fairly modest house but it was ours. A young girl named Judy lived next door. She was still at high school but become another valuable employee. We had also hired two or three other girls but Margaret and Annette remained the backbone of the staff, along of course, with Gaye.

Annette's sisters Robyn and Jenny would also help out on a part time basis. Like Annette, they were real gems and we got to be friends with all their family and whenever Annette wanted time off she would have a sister to take her place. Then when Robyn wanted time off when she had a baby she also had a sister to take her place. When Jenny left who is the third sister to get married I jokingly said "I know you have run out of sisters so when does your mum start?". She just laughed but I had met her Mum and I knew she would've been good in the shop.

All these people are lifelong friends along with Jeanette Van Beam and Lee Veralo. These were to follow in years to come. Watching these girls grow up, get married and have children is really something. Margaret in particular is very special and we are very close to her even after all these years.

Annette Margaret and Gaye at Margaret's wedding

CHAPTER 11

FRIENDS

The best part of this period in time wasn't only the fact that at last we had some spare cash and didn't have to watch our pennies any more, it was that we had made some great friends which would mean more to us than any amount of money.

The manager of a men's clothing store which was situated next to my shop was to become a great friend. Mal Avery and I hit it off right away. We were to have some great times and are still very close. Unfortunately, we live a distance from each other, the one and possibly only down side of me living in Augusta. Mal still works in the rag trade and is married to a lovely lady and I mean lady, her name is Val.

Gaye with Judi 1990

Val Jill and Gaye

Mal is so important to my life that I am going to give him his own segment in this story. He's going to be wrapped in that and he deserves it and I'm sure it will be the first thing he will look for if he ever gets to read this book. I have a million stories about Mal, most of them about little situations he seems to get himself into. He is a very forgiving person and I like to tell Mal's stories. He doesn't seem to mind as he knows we all love him. It's just part of Mal's character. We met some wonderful friends because of Mal, first there was his wife Val and her friend Judi, then Sandi and her husband Jim and Lee Hunt and her many boyfriends. I hope Lee can take a joke!! Let's just say she is very popular but slightly difficult at times.

Jill and Mike; Pauline and Peter; Susie Farrell, as she was known then, and lots of others too numerous to mention. Some of them have gone their various ways but the people I have mentioned here are still very strong friends. I have been with them when they have been married, had children, good and bad times, break-ups and everything else along the way. They have been likewise to Gaye and I and have been with us through our many ups and downs and we still all stick together.

Firstly Judi, I wasn't sure when we first met her whether she was Mal's girlfriend or not. Anyway, Mal married Val and Judi married Phil. I can recall when Judi accompanied us on a holiday to Albany, this was before she was married. Lisa and Graeme were only young and loved listening to Judi's stories. One about the wide mouthed frog had to be told over and over again as the kids' were spellbound.

On this trip, which was at Easter time, Gaye and Judi went to Church as all good girls should do at this time of the year. When the congregation went on a march through the streets of Albany, following Jesus on the cross, Gaye and Judi had to join in. They followed for a while but when they thought no-one was looking they ducked off down a back street to have a smoke, only to run headlong into the Minister and Jesus again. I guess he must've blessed them for all their sins.

It was on this trip that we first heard about the mysterious Phil. Some weeks later we met him at Val and Mal's unit in Scarborough. We were watching the English Soccer FA Cup and were all singing the Sunderlands Theme Song, something about red, red robin!! It was like we had known Phil all our lives. I remember Val had made a lovely dinner of scallops. I told you I had a good memory and the dinner was lovely!

Judi and Phil joined us on a great Asian trip with the Manilla hotel a highlight. The overthrow of the Marcos' was happening before our very eyes. Ferdinand and Imelda had thrown a wonderful party at the hotel and we were guests. I guess he just wanted to go out in style.

Phil and I had some wonderful times going to the VFL Grand Finals and staying at the majestic Windsor Hotel. Phil and I staged a wrestling match in our room and the old antique furniture was a bit fragile! Murray Cutbush was in the room at the time watching old VFL Grand Final replays. He was pretty worried about it getting out of hand but it didn't and we told him afterwards that he could've put the damage bill on Bondy's account, after all he was picking up the tab for our lunches and dinners on his expense account. Alan could afford it at the time, there was no doubt about that!

Sandi and Jim were and still are very special. I first met them when we were living in Como. We would go out to dinner and then the whole group would go back to their place and party on. Lots of dancing and a few drinks. Gaye didn't drink so she was always the skipper. Their next home was a lovely old place in Fremantle. They now live on a farm in the Pinjarra area. We are always welcome but visit too infrequently. Sandi and I have always been close but I have also had plenty of good times with Jim. He would join us on some of our VFL Grand Final trips with some memorable moments with after match parties at some of our friends' places.

My first memory of Lee was of watching football. She followed Subiaco while Judi and Jill were West Perth supporters. I followed Perth. I can remember being introduced to her at the football. "Lee Hunt you say? I happen to have a sister Lea Hunt, although she is now Lea Robertson.". But this Lee Hunt has stuck to her guns, even after a multitude of relationships, she is still good old Lee Hunt, this shows you what class this girl has. Early memories of Lee were her ability to break out into a ballet dance at the slightest encouragement. One or two drinks and off she would go. Her daughter Danielle would've been proud of her as Dani is no slouch when it comes to ballet.

Jill was always the life of the party. I can remember one New Years Day at the Perth Cup, it was very, very hot as it usually is on this day but Jill wasn't thirsty though as she had a couple or ten champagnes, she was hot though so she sat in the ice container, it wasn't a wet t-shirt it was a wet, see-through dress. I would like to say it wasn't a pretty sight but I can assure you it certainly was.

Pauline is a good friend of Val's and I've often wondered what would've happened if Mal had married Pauline. It's a scary thought, Mal and Pauline are so much alike that it would more than likely have been unworkable. Pauline was married to Bobby and they had two lovely boys. This union didn't last for all that long, however, and she was single for a while and then married Peter.

I can remember when she was single and we were on holiday with Sandi and Jim down at Peaceful Bay. Tom had a holiday house at Peaceful Bay and he was generous enough to let us holiday there on more than one occasion. We'd had a great time as we usually did and were on our way back home to Perth. Pauline had a little, old car that was prone to breakdowns and it was decided that I would follow her home in my car. She had a faulty carburettor and the jet would sometimes stick causing the car to stall with petrol pouring out everywhere. The car would then be hard to restart. Everything seemed to be OK once it was running but the carby would flood every time she stopped. I told her that the best thing to do was not to stop. That seemed obvious.

We got going but down the road a bit she stopped!! I pulled up behind her and said "What's wrong?". "All's OK" she said, "we just needed to go to the toilet and this seemed like a good spot". No use telling her that it was usually a good idea to go before you set out on a long trip. We only just got the car started before the battery went completely flat. Down the road a bit she stopped again, I wasn't impressed "What's wrong now?". "Nothing, the boys wanted an ice-cream and I'm not sure if there are any more shops for a while." she said. Gaye, myself and even little Lisa and Graeme managed to push her fast enough to start the car. I said "Don't even think about stopping again." and we sailed along happily for quite a distance and you guessed it, she stopped again. I was furious. "What's wrong now?" I demanded. "I'm finding it hard to concentrate" she said "the boys are playing up and I just need a rest." I said "I'll give you a rest, if you stop again I'll wring your pretty little neck, get it?" She said, "Don't be angry Cubby", she called me Cubby for some unknown reason, "we are on holidays you should be happy". We pushed the car again and I told her at this rate she would run out of petrol or even worse the car could catch fire as petrol was pouring out of it. Anyway, we got back to Perth and there were no more incidents and everyone was happy. I'm sure Pauline didn't even think about it the next day, she was home safe and sound.

Mal

Mal seems to get himself into situations, most times when he is trying to do the right thing. Because of this, Karma seems to be on his side. He gets himself out of these situations most times as the cards seem to fall his way. He is a great mate, a very loyal and upbeat person.

As I mentioned before, I first met Mal in the early days of Garden City when he managed the Menswear store next to my shop. We hit it off straight away, firstly playing squash after work and then Mal sometimes would come back to our place, staying overnight and sleeping on the couch. We had some great times together, trips to Rottnest Island, many trips over to Melbourne, mostly to watch the VFL Grand Finals and also just socialising with our other friends, attending weddings, parties, card nights, etc.

On one occasion we drove across the Nullarbor in my GT Falcon and stayed at Gaye's sister and brother-in-law, Wendy and Graeme's place, they were great hosts but I'm sure they would sigh with relief when we left. One night Wendy said that they were going to their daughter's Kindergarten fundraiser and asked if we wanted to come. Mal and I looked at each other and made a few excuses, it sounded a bit boring to us. Graeme said "It's usually a fun night and the neighbours are going as well". Graeme was a straight shooter, if he said it would be fun, we would go.

There weren't many men there, just a lot of young Mums, I guess their husbands had thought it would be boring as well! Mal and I were in great demand as dancing partners. We lapped up the attention and afterwards attended a party over the road from Wendy's place. We came away from the party with some lunch invitations for the next day. Wendy said "forget about it, I can't do much about Mal as he isn't married but you're grounded." Graeme thought it was a great joke. We also attended a couple of great nights at the local golf club.

Every time I went East, Gaye would give me lots of instructions, I would have to visit all of our relatives, this was only right but there were a lot of them so I would just have to do my best. First there were her parents, I knew where they lived, I had been there hundreds of times. We pulled up in the driveway and as the back door was open we went inside, calling out "surprise, surprise". No-one was home, however, I said to Mal "they can't be far away, they wouldn't leave the back door open". Everything was how I remembered it, I hadn't been there for a few years but the furniture was the same, it was all familiar. We made ourselves at home, after all, they were family. I put the kettle on and Mal was looking at the family photos on the mantelpiece. "Not many photos of Gaye, I can't see any as a matter of fact." He said. "They've probably taken them down as punishment for marrying me." I joked. We had our cup of tea and turned the telly on. Mal was curled up on the couch so I thought I would check the photos out. Not only weren't there any of Gaye, there were none of the rest of the family. It was an entirely different family. It was then that the penny dropped, I said to Mal, "Come on, we are going". He said "No we can stay a bit longer if you like". I dragged him out and slapped the Falcon in reverse and sped out down the road to the next street where Gaye's parents were home. I said to Mal "Don't mention this to anyone". He was still trying to figure it all out.

No trip to Melbourne without a visit to Gaye's big sister Patti's place. We had a dinner invitation, but first we would spend the afternoon with some of Mal's friends. We overstayed and Mal wasn't in a very good condition. By the time we arrived it was nearly 10pm. We pulled up in the drive which was on a bit of a slope. Mal fell out of the car and rolled down the drive, he was clutching some bottles of wine which we'd bought on the way as a peace offering. Mal had done a good job of not breaking the wine. The patio light went on and Patti's husband, Gigi, came out. He wasn't impressed.

We went inside and Patti was very welcoming. I introduced Mal who was trying his best to act normal but could hardly speak. We sat down to dinner, the kids Janine, who was 10 or 12 and Marc who was a bit younger had finished their meal. Mal muttered something about not being hungry and just stood with his back to the wall for support. I was driving so hadn't had anything to drink but Mal's condition was deteriorating, he was sliding down the wall. Patti said "maybe he'd like to lie down for a while?", Mal just nodded. I said "yes, he's a bit tired", after all he'd had a late night the night before.

Gaye with her Mum and Dad also brother Ken.

Gaye with her sisters, Patti, Vivian and Wendy

Wendy with her daughters Melissa and Sallyanne at
Janine's wedding on the 9th of April, 1994

Gaye with Vivians daughter Emma and Jock

John and Annetta

Where to put Mal was debated by Gigi and Patti, the only bed available was Janine's. Gigi who was of Italian heritage was having none of it, "He isn't sleeping in my little girl's bed". He did make it into her bed however and Janine thought it was a great joke. How we later got Mal up and going I'm not sure. Needless to say Mal was never invited back.

Mal loved my car and driving over he couldn't wait for his turn to drive. I would rest but would keep one eye open as Mal's sense of direction is non-existent. I would be worried that Mal would take the wrong turn on the Eyre Highway, not that you could of course, there was only east or west, no other turnoffs but with Mal driving one couldn't be too careful. On arriving in Melbourne he said, I will take the car through the carwash if you like as it was very dusty. When he arrived back, the car wasn't all that soggy inside, he had managed to close the sunroof before the interior was completely flooded. Thank goodness for leather seats and the carpet wasn't all that wet!

One night Mal asked if he could borrow the car to go into the city to see his friend Bobby Hannah who was recording his TV show, Blind Date. Bobby was later to marry Pauline. I said to Mal "Are you sure you know the way?" Graeme gave him a street directory and he said

"No sweat, it's in Fitzroy, I know where that is". He said he wouldn't be long. The show finishes at 8.30 and he would be home by 9.30 at the latest. Graeme and I sat up waiting for him to get home a bit like anxious parents. At about 11.00 pm, we were getting a bit worried. At 12.00 midnight, panic had set in. At 1.00 am we were ready to call the police when headlights appeared in the driveway, followed by another set of lights. I was sure it was the Police. No, it was a taxi, apparently the taxi driver had seen Mal driving past his taxi rank a few times then Mal stopped and asked directions to Templestowe. Not long after Mal drove past again, the Taxi driver stopped him and offered to escort him home. Mal just thought "Well, that was nice of him wasn't it, I knew the way but just got stuck on a roundabout."

A more recent story happened a few years ago, Mal and Val had invited Gaye and I to spend a week at their house in Dawesville. I brought some fresh Augusta whiting that Graeme and I had caught. Mal and I would cook it on their BBQ which was situated on the patio. On the way inside, Mal dropped the dish of fish batter, he was onto it in a flash, mopping it up before Val saw it.

In the morning we were to go for a drive into Mandurah to look at a block of land they had just bought. Val, Gaye and I waited out the front while Mal went to get the car which was in the carport around the back. After about 10 minutes or so Val said "bloody Mal, he has no idea how to back the car out!" We walked around the back only to see Mal up on the roof of Val's new Honda. "What the hell are you doing?" said Val, Mal was trying to scramble down and make himself invisible. Val then spotted the rag in his hand and then said "Mal, you're a darling, I knew I shouldn't have parked under that tree yesterday, bird shit is terrible to get off, it can mark the paint permanently". I thought to myself "not as bad as batter though, it sets like concrete". I just chuckled to myself, Mal had come out of it smelling like roses as he normally does. I doubt if Val ever knows the truth to this day!! She may if she reads the book I suppose.

We visited Rottnest Island regularly and on one occasion we had to spend the night on the beach due to bad weather. Coming back the next day the weather really closed in, all boating traffic had apparently been banned. We ran out of fuel just inside Fremantle. It was getting dark and waves were starting to wash over the boat.

We let off some flares and when nothing happened we thought we will have to try and spend the night in the boat. We had Graeme with us, I guess he was only about 10 at the time. Luckily the Sea Rescue saw us and towed us back to safety. I was the Skipper and must take full responsibility for this and it could've ended in disaster.

Val and Mal often house sat for us in those early days. On one occasion when Gaye, Graeme and myself went to New Zealand for a couple of weeks, they moved in and looked after Lisa. We really appreciated that.

John Hiskins, Ray Litis and Ron Walters were three of my best friends of all time. I met them first through playing football with Victoria Park and later on when our playing days were finished, we continued our friendship. John and Ray would attend matches with the Perth Football Club in the WAFL and we would have great times afterwards.

One of the highlights of our friendship was a trip to Tasmania to watch the 1981 Interdominion Trotting Championships. There was a local horse competing called San Simeon who was stabled just around the corner from my property in Byford and we knew the trainer/driver, Lou Austin. Upon arriving in Hobart, we looked around for a bookmaker. In those days Hobart only had freelance bookmakers, I'd been to Tassie before and knew this. We asked about San Simeon, no-one seemed to know who the heck this horse was. Not being punters but thinking that San Simeon was unbeatable, we immediately backed him and got some good odds. Needless to say, San Simeon won the final of the race and this win virtually paid for our whole trip.

We also met another friend of John's at the races, I forget his name so I'll just call him Gary, he was a really colourful character and he introduced us to his local hotel where we had some great meals. We did a tour of Tasmania in a hire car and then in between the last heat of the interdominion and the final, we decided to have a short trip to

Melbourne to meet Kevin Sheedy whose mother was a friend of John's mother.

We had a great night out, even had a couple of hours in a nightclub. Kevin had just been appointed coach of Essendon, it was his first year and it was really great of him to give us that night out. Upon arrival back in Hobart, Gary informed us that the police wanted to see us, apparently the night we left to go to Melbourne, the hotel which we had been hanging out in had been robbed and of course we were the prime suspects. We'd only just arrived in Hobart and spent most of our time in this pub and this Gary was a pretty colourful character. He'd introduced us to all sorts of people at the races, the Police Commissioner and some pretty dodgy characters. We immediately thought that it was a set up, that this guy had robbed the hotel and we're the ones who're going to take the blame but as it turned out they caught the robbers and it had nothing to do with Gary and we were in the clear. That was a great trip and John and Ray still remain very good friends of mine.

My Great Mate Ron

I first met Ron when we were playing football with Victoria Park. He lived close by and we hit it off immediately. We had a lot of common interests, football, horses, fishing and our families, which became great friends. He had a daughter Kelly and a son Glen much the same ages as my Lisa and Graeme. Ron was a person that everyone loved, he never had a bad word to say about anyone. We both had a love of horses and dreamt of owning a champion, we would go to the yearling sales every year and this would make our wives extremely nervous, not knowing what we would come home with. Sometimes we weren't too sure ourselves. We had some good horses though, Red Marshall and Racy Storm won a lot of races and I bred another horse that Ron got off me called White Water and he was progressing extremely well. Our first horse was a horse called Young Pedro, he was very, very slow unfortunately.

Good mate Ron on his boat at Rottnest

Ray and John also had a horse called Al's Vision which I was a partner in as well. He was a similar horse to Young Pedro, he would just run along with his mates, not wanting to pass them, just run along with them. Al's Vision, however, did win Horse of the Year at Wagin which I suppose was a bit of a minor achievement.

Ron bought a property not far from mine and we put some cattle on his and my place. I guess we thought ourselves as being mini cattle barons and we dreamed about one day having big farms. Of course this never eventuated. We also went on quite a few fishing trips on Ron's boat to Rottnest Island and also to the Abrolhos Islands. On one trip to the Abrolhos Islands we nearly got shipwrecked when the motor conked out on Ron's boat. We drifted for a while and this was very alarming as the compass was also broken. Ron's toolbox consisted of a pressure can of magic spray. He got it out and said "If this doesn't work

I'm not sure what we're going to do." It did work and we got going again and had a great time.

I went through some bad times with Ron, first was his marriage break up, this really affected him badly, but worse was to come. One Christmas, he was just jogging on the beach one morning which he normally did, as he liked to keep himself fit and he had a heart attack and died. This was unbelievable to me as I had been with him the night before and he seemed quite OK. His girlfriend Anna came up to my property the next day and broke the news to me, we simply couldn't believe it.

This was also compounded by Margaret's husband Mike who was also a good friend and was much the same age in his 40s and he died of cancer the following Christmas. I still miss Ron big time, he was a great friend.

CHAPTER 12

CHARLES GAYE JEWELLERS PART B

There was good news and bad news. My father passed away at this time which was very sad of course. Mum and Dad had retired to Rosebud on the Mornington Penninsula, he was only in his early 70s. I went to Melbourne to attend his funeral and around about this time Gaye's Mum also passed away. Dad suffered from heart problems late in life but his death was a real shock. The Hunt men all seem to have this problem and his brothers all died far too early with heart related illnesses, then again everyone smoked in those days. I try and look after my heart and my doctor keeps an eye on it and of course I don't smoke.

The shop was going well, but there was trouble ahead. At our good friend Wendy's party one night at Bull Creek, I don't whether it was to celebrate another marriage or a divorce, there is a fair bit of activity in this department at this particular time with Wendy's marital affairs, the Police called at about midnight asking for me, there had been a major break in at the Shopping Centre with my shop as the target.

I was stunned and heartbroken when I saw the shop. Glass smashed everywhere, still some jewellery lying around in the Mall. Where had the security staff been and what about the alarms? We were an inside shop, they had to smash the front doors down as well as my windows. This may well have destroyed us but we did survive. The bank helped out and even a customer, a little old lady who said she would bankroll me to whatever I needed, no interest, no limit on time to pay her back. She had no family and I had been good to her as I had made a lot of jewellery for her. I thanked her but in the end we didn't need to take her up on her kind offer. Later on, I found out that she was a famous Madam but a very kind hearted one, a lovely lady.

I was insured, but only covered for the stock in the safe. It wasn't possible to put the whole shop in the safe, big as it was. They never caught the robbers and neither did I get any stock back but in a twist of fate six months later there was a fatal car smash in the hills out of Perth. Apparently there was jewellery everywhere in the car, none of it mine worst luck, but the main person of interest in my robbery was killed, bad luck about that I suppose, he got his just deserts. I wasn't crying.

Jeweller Charles Hunt examines
a window broken in the Booragoon raid

This appeared on the front page of Perth's morning newspaper,
The West Australian

Another problem was to surface in the shape of the Australian Taxation Office. I had formed a wholesale jewellery company as the buying arm of Charles Gaye. Sales Tax was 33% on jewellery and I was expected to pay this immediately as part of the purchase price when I bought stock from manufacturers, even though it may take years to sell at retail. This wasn't really fair. When we sold the jewellery we would then pay the sales tax, this seemed fair and was legal in the eyes of my accountants.

The ATO didn't like it and slapped me with a heavy fine and stiff interest penalties for the longer I took to pay the fine. I refused to pay and the amount owing was becoming very serious indeed. I had some inside information however, Lisa's boyfriend at the time, Greg, was in a senior position at the ATO, not in the Sales Tax Division but he had access to my case. He told me that they were very nervous. We had hired a taxation lawyer who said we were 100% right. The ATO didn't want to go to court because if they lost, all jewellers would follow my lead and this would put a dent in the ATO's cash flow.

We had a meeting with the enemy, the outcome being I would pay a token fine only. They would save face and continue on their merry way. It was a huge load off my mind.

There were to be big changes to the Shopping Centre, it was to be expanded to make it more than twice the size. There were also to be changes to the Centre rental agreements. On top of the base rent, a percentage rental was to be added, meaning that you would pay a percentage of your turnover to the Management. This was completely against my thinking and it would penalise the successful stores and help the lame ducks. To improve the Centre, surely all stores should be encouraged to be successful. Nevertheless, owners were queuing up to get into the Centre. I was approached from a leading city jeweller who wanted to buy my shop. It had a good location and he wasn't taking any chances on obtaining a new shop in the expansion. It was food for thought.

I'd built a shed on my property and was spending weekends there playing with my horses and cattle. Graeme, who was attending Wesley College, wanted to train horses, he was no scholar and was working part-time with Bill Warwick, learning about horses. I was friends with all the Warwick family and Bill's friend, Colin was to drive my horses in years to come. Gaye and I talked it over. "What will you do if you sell?" she asked. I wasn't sure, "I guess I'm just sick of being a jeweller. You get robbed, Centre Management now wants to take any that the robbers have missed and then the ATO will take whatever crumbs are left over, it just doesn't make sense." That look came back on Gaye's face, this time it wasn't "idiot", it was "Have you really lost your mind?

You mean you'll sell the shop and do nothing, is that the plan?". "Yeah, sort of" I said.

Gaye was loving being a jeweller and who could blame her, she could model the jewellery and some of it never seemed to make it's way back into stock, also cash was no problem for her. Nearly every night I would find a little note in the till "$150 out signed Gaye", "$200 out signed Gaye" and so on. When I questioned her about this she would say "Well, if I don't put a note in there how are you going to balance the books?". "Very thoughtful of you, but what are you doing with the money?" I asked. "Housekeeping, Stupid" was the reply "Anyway, you don't pay me a wage so I have to pay myself." Gaye has always deep down resented leaving her family in Melbourne and at last she seemed settled. She was working part time in a health studio/gymnasium and had qualified as an instructor. She seemed to love this work and she was looking good and healthy. Byford is too far away from Como where the health studio was located so she said "I will have to give that up I suppose. I could work with Alan Linney.". Alan now had a business in the Armadale Pioneer Village which wasn't too far away from the farm. "Good idea" I said, thinking well at least one of us would be earning a living.

I promised to build her a nice big house on the property and even showed her some designs. She could have whatever she wanted. My best mate Ron had his own building company and I knew lots of tradesmen in the football club, bricklayers, plumbers, carpenters, etc. I would get an owner/builder permit and build the house myself. That would be the least of our worries, we would save thousands. Ron would supervise the building to make sure it was all A1.

Tom was a major concern though, what would he do? He was happy to retire, I would pay him a good redundancy package and he was happy. Margaret and Annette weren't a concern they had been married for some time and had families and no longer worked. I had a new head woman called Vivien and she would relocate and buy her own business in Busselton. This wasn't a problem so we sold.

CHAPTER 13

LISA GOES GLOBAL

With a friend Alex and barely 18, she was off to see the world. She had saved a fair amount of money which she would leave with me with strict instructions not to send any of it unless she was absolutely desperate. Only once did she need any of it as most of the time she paid her way working at various jobs. On the first night in London, staying at a Backpackers, she got a job there. Most of the day was spent sightseeing and she could stay in the hostel as long as she liked as long as she helped out.

Alex and her then bought some bikes and cycled around the south of England still not spending much money. Helping farmers, in return sleeping in their barns and getting meals. Lisa then travelled by ferry to Belgium to meet old friends who lived in Luxembourg, she spent the winter with Attilio and Charmaine, they had a jewellery shop in Luxembourg and had both worked for me in my shops when they were in Perth. Their son Roger, was an Optometrist and started the optometry chain Just Spectacles. They were a very clever family, watch makers, jewellers and optometrists, never met anyone with all those combined skills before.

Attilio was also a pilot and took Lisa flying over France, Italy and Switzerland. They were very good to her and we were relieved that she was safe in their hands. However, she was then accepted to live and work on a Kibbutz in Israel. The hostilities between Israel and Egypt were at boiling point but this didn't stop Lisa from hitchhiking to Cairo one day then back to the Kibbutz, getting a lift with some Israeli soldiers.

We were getting used to receiving phone calls at all hours of the night, it would be Lisa, saying "I'm in Paris, isn't that great?". It was great, just to hear her voice. It was about this time that Gaye and I had our first separation. I moved out and rented an apartment in South Perth. We continued to work together as if nothing had happened and the separation didn't last all that long. We were soon back together again. We were living a hectic life and I guess there was a fair amount of stress involved on both sides. I was away a fair bit of the time on buying trips in Melbourne and Gaye was left to manage the shop along with Tom of course.

We had sold our house in Stirk Road, Alfred Cove and had bought a small acreage in Byford, somewhere to keep my horses. We then rented a house in Ardross, just around the corner from the shop.

CHAPTER 14

MY AMERICAN TRIP PART 1

While I was waiting to get my owner/builder permit approved from the Shire of Serpentine/Jarrahdale, I decided to take a trip to America to sell some opals. We had some left over from the shop and the price of opals in America was a lot better than Australia.

My first stop was Honolulu, where I checked things out, got some good tips and made good contacts for Los Angeles. I liked Hawaii, the people were nice and it would've been nice to have had the time to explore some of the other islands.

I headed to LA. I'd booked a room at the Hilton in downtown LA. It was over 30 years ago so it's a bit hazy, however, I remember the room well. They had asked me if I'd like a suite at the same price as a room, of course I would! It was a triangular broom closet in the corner of the hotel and everything was in miniature! Lucky I am fairly small and being very tired after my long flight I went to sleep right away. I was jolted out of bed by an almighty roar at 4.30 am, looked out of the window and thought I'd been transported to the middle of the freeway. There were on ramps and off ramps above and below, they seemed to be intertwined with the hotel. I was on about the twelfth floor and there were more ramps above me and the noise was deafening.

I took a taxi to the opal buyers and did some business after which I decided to walk back to my hotel as it was only a few blocks away and I could actually see the hotel. Big, big mistake!! I wandered into a locality which seemed like the back streets of Mexico or Brasil. There were bodies in doorways and on the footpath, I didn't know if they were dead or alive! There were gangs of four or five people everywhere all eyeing me off. I was in a business suit with a small clutch bag of opals. I stood out amongst these guys, they could've killed me and nobody would've known. In fact I thought they were going to kill me.

I looked around for a taxi but there wasn't even any traffic, I think even taxi drivers were too scared to venture into this area. There were no shops open anywhere, just seedy bars, tattoo parlours and any shops had been boarded up. There were no "normal" people anywhere!! At last I spotted two construction workers erecting a sign and they directed me to where I could get a taxi.

I was out of LA by bus the next day on my way to Vegas. LA, they can stick it! However, I did have to go back as I had an appointment with the same opal guys. This time I booked into an apartment somewhere near Beverley Hills, not the real posh area but nice enough to be able to walk around the streets.

When I went back to the opal guys, they told me that they all carry guns otherwise they would be held up every day. They said that the people who had been in the area would've thought that I had a gun in my little clutch bag. That was what saved me, as no-one would be brazen enough to walk around in their patch without one!

On The Buses, American Style

I decided a day at the beach would be pleasant, after all you can't visit California without visiting the famous Santa Monica Pier! I checked out where to get the bus and what number it was. A straight trip along Wiltshire Boulevard, a long way but I had all day. I joined the queue with a $5 note in my hand, it was a fair amount of money so it should cover the fare. I wasn't too sure of the rules but passengers were putting tickets in the little box near the driver, some were putting cash in so I felt at ease. When it came to my turn I asked the 6'7" African American bus driver "How much to the beach?". No answer but I figured that once we got going he would attend to me.

People got on, people got off, at four or five different stops but still no answer. I was left standing there, I asked the giant driver "This bus does go to the Pier I hope?". Still no answer! At this stage, people were starting to take notice so I turned to them, someone will help this poor little Aussie guy surely?? No-one would make eye contact, they had stopped talking amongst themselves. They could recognise trouble, it was in their DNA. I tried the giant again in a quiet, meek voice. Well, I didn't want everyone to think that I was a troublemaker. "Please sir I would like to pay my fare." "There is no change on the buses", he barked at me and also muttered something about "dumbass". I'm sure the passengers thought "this is it, this is where the strange talking guy takes out the giant".

They could smell fear, even I could smell it, I wasn't sure what to do. I thought about getting off the bus and walking home but figured I would get mugged for sure, so I stuffed my $5 in the box. I would've gladly put $20 in but I didn't want to fumble around in my wallet, someone might've thought I was going for a gun and taken me out. "Shoot first and ask questions later", would be their motto. Anyway, I had no trouble finding a seat, most of the people had moved right to the back of the bus!

Another incident happened when I was on my way to Nevada to visit Los Vegas. However, I guess this story is fairly normal as I was the only one who seemed concerned! We stopped in an LA suburb to pick up some passengers. A young Hispanic woman got on followed by about half a dozen or so family or friends I guess. They then tried to drag her off the bus. They were shouting and fighting and this went on for a good 20 minutes. They were getting on the bus they were getting off the bus, they were pushing and shoving and it started to get pretty ugly. Nobody else seemed concerned, they all continued reading. The bus driver got out of his cab and sat down on the seat next to the bus stop. I said to the woman next to me "Shouldn't someone call the police?". She replied "no, they will sort it out themselves." Of course they did and off we went. Strange place, LA!!

CHAPTER 15

BUILDING THE HOUSE

Building had started on the new house. The property was very pretty with lots of large gum trees and there as a permanent creek crossing the property so we decided to build the house close-by. First I had to build a long driveway so the trucks could bring in sand for the foundations. Then the concrete slab was laid. Next came the brick layers and this was the start of the headaches. I had ordered the wrong brickie sand, he would only work with one type of sand. I said "get over it, it looks OK to me". Peter was a personal friend of mine but that didn't matter, his sand was so special to him he refused to work until I got the right sand for him. Fully imported from some obscure sandpit but I had no choice.

Gaye cooking for Keith and Lea before the house was built

Then the second headache, Peter informed me that the slab was too big, according to the plans "no problem" I said "just make everything bigger". He said "I can do that but you don't know what headaches you will have in store for you down the track". "OK, just go ahead, it'll be OK" I said. It wasn't just a case of ordering more bricks though, the roof timbers wouldn't fit, the windows wouldn't fit and so on. I had visions of sitting back at home with my feet up while the tradies did their job. Wrong. I was run ragged, checking on everything, changing things, visiting suppliers, co-ordinating the job, if the tradies turned up for work and things weren't to their liking, they would just leave and getting them back was challenging.

Finally the house was finished. John Hiskins was a landscape gardener and he did the brick paving for me. I did the painting myself, I could handle that. Some years later, a few rooms were still unpainted but I did finish most of it before we moved in.

Mum's visit to the farm. Gaye, Glen, Lea and Mum

Mum and Lea

It was a beautiful house. John and Ray would come up at weekends and help me build stables and horseyards. We had lots of interstate visitors in the next few months, first Gaye's dad, Jock, he was an ex-jockey so he just adored the horses. I just wished my Dad was still alive, he also loved horses and would've been very proud. Next, Gaye's sister Patti with her family Gigi, Janine and Mark. Then a visit from my sisters, Lea and Glen, who had a great surprise for me, they had my Mum with them. I hadn't had a lot of close contact with these guys for some time, funerals, weddings and rushed business trips didn't do a lot for family bonding. I really appreciated Mum being there, she was elderly but in good health and I'm sure she really enjoyed herself.

Next, another of Gaye's sisters arrived, Vivian, she brought her two daughters with her, Emma who was only a baby and Jody, a teenager. They stayed for some time and then settled in WA. It was about this time that Graeme relocated to Coffs Harbour. He was to stay there for some years, finally coming back and helping me with the horses and then later my food shops. It was good to get him home.

CHAPTER 16

HORSES

This period of my life was without doubt the most exciting. Except of course for my wedding day, the birth of my children, Lisa's wedding day and the birth of my grandsons!!

Horses are fun, lots of work, very expensive to keep and heartbreaking at times. We've always had animals in our life. Growing up in Redcliffs, we had plenty of them, in Carlton I kept chickens in our tiny backyard much to Dad's anguish because we had a food shop and it just wasn't something you did in Carlton, but I did! We've had lots of dogs, too numerous to mention, Graeme also loved animals and as most young boys do. He had a bug collection and all sorts of animals from guinea pigs to goldfish. He loved the horses and couldn't wait to leave school so he could be with them all day. My only contact with horses had been when I was about ten and Dad would hand the reigns over to me when we would be out delivering vegetables in Redcliffs. We had a lovely grey horse called Barney, he was so quiet, he didn't even really need a driver.

Ron and I decided one day we would like a horse of our own. We were regularly attending the trotting races at Gloucester Park, along with our friends John and Ray. When we lived in Preston, Dad would take me and a couple of my mates to the trots on a Saturday night at the old Melbourne showgrounds so guess trotting was in my blood.

Ron and I studied the yearling catalogues and picked out a future champion and off we went and bought him. Once buying him we had no idea what to do with him. This was pre-Byford property days, we both lived in suburbia. We gave the horse to a trainer but our high hopes were dashed as he couldn't run out of sight on a dark night. This didn't deter us, however and we bought a couple more the following year but with the same result. We weren't aware that 90% of the horses that are sold in these sales never even make it to the track.

My next purchase was a lovely little horse named Star Effect. He had a white star on his nice chestnut forehead so the name of Star was obvious. He won quite a few races, mostly in the country so the next year, Ron and I bought his brother which we named Red Marshall. Red had heaps of ability but was very erratic and three or four trainers gave up on him until he at last settled down. He went on to win a lot of races, mainly in the city, he had a tragic ending to his life which I might talk about later.

Myself and stable hand Kirsty. I'm holding" Bluey", my champ.

A Winner in Perth

Me at the beach with Racy Storm

I was studying horse breeding and when I noticed Star Effect and Red's dam, Sarah, was up for sale I had to have her. She was old but had classic breeding and her first foal in New Zealand was a champion. By this time we were living on the property so I would breed with Sarah. My plan was taking shape, I would breed horses and sell them in the yearling sales. I would make a fortune. The shoe would on the other foot, I would be the vendor. I sent Sarah to a top American stallion called Romeo Hanover, it was a great combination with the result being a lovely chestnut colt. I would put him in the yearling sales and he surely would bring a pretty penny.

There was plenty of interest in him and the bidding soon reached $10,000 a good price in those days. In fact it was in the top 10% of sales on the day. I had a reserve of $14,000 however, so he was passed in. There were plenty of trainers who were still interested in looking at him after the sales some said "surely $10,000 would have to buy him?". I arrived home with both Gaye and Bluey (Bluey was the name I had given him. It's an Aussie thing, redheads are called Bluey so that name was obvious). Gaye wasn't talking to me, she was speechless, $10,000 would've been a welcome addition to our dwindling finances. It was quite obvious I was in love with Bluey.

Hey Maybe

"Follow your heart" I said to Gaye "that's what life's all about". This horse is a champion, I can feel the vibes, he just has that look in his eye. He was to go to Bill Warwick for his initial training, Graeme was still working with Bill and the reports coming home each night weren't encouraging. "He can't even pace" Graeme would say and "Bill thinks he is a dud." Pacing is a basic requirement of any pacer, he of course isn't a trotter, he is a pacer. "Bill says he is very dopey, he's all looks with no ability". It looked like he would be sent home back to me and what to do with him would be a problem. Much like the problem I had with Gaye who wasn't impressed.

Hey Maybe, Bluey, my champion

However, things started to turn around, he was beginning to get the hang of it. He was still very young. Bill took him to the two year old trials at Gloucester Park and he bolted in. He would have his first start at Pinjarra and we would be up against the best two years olds in WA. Bluey ran third after being blocked for a clear run, he still wasn't two years of age yet as he was born in December and horses have their birthdays on 1 August. He was giving most of them two or three months head start.

Two weeks later he was to start in a race at Gloucester Park. He won easily, in fact he won at his next four starts and was now rated as the best two year old in the West. His race name was Hey Maybe and he had certainly answered that question.

After a slight break in training he was to have a bad accident on the training track, he fell and injured both his front knees. It had come at a bad time as all the big two year old races were coming up. Bill said it wasn't a serious injury he could still race him, he would treat his knees and he would be OK. He was to start in the first two year old classic of the season and was a red hot favourite even though he had a bad barrier draw. He got badly blocked for a clear run again and couldn't get out of the pocket until the race was virtually all over. He finished third. I was disappointed but worse was to follow.

He could hardly walk off the track. He had broken down badly in one of his front legs. We should've rested him until his knees healed. That was in hindsight of course. I took him home and treated his injured leg with an expensive magneto pulse machine I had bought. After some months rest his leg looked good but Bill wasn't keen to have him back. He said "I have never seen a horse come back any good with a bad suspensory ligament injury". I gave him to another trainer who said we would take him to the beach for training, which would help his legs.

Bluey started in the Rich Western Gateway Stakes at the Old Fremantle Track, Richmond Raceway. It was the first major three year old race of the season and in fact it was his first start with a new trainer. He bolted in and won his next five starts, he was officially a champion. Next was the WA Derby, the major three year old race. He was a red hot favourite again. Even though the best horses were in the race he appeared to have it at his mercy. He was a very fast beginner and whenever he led he was never beaten. He led in this race! It was pressured in front by another horse, it was team driving as the stable had another horse in the race and they were going to set it up for this other horse. He was to be run ragged and be a sitting duck at the finish but he still led with 100 metres to go and finished fifth.

Worse was to come, he had broken down badly this time with a cracked sesamoid bone in his opposite front leg. He couldn't walk and had to be almost lifted into the horse float to go home. I was furious, not at losing the race but the fact that they had ruined a lovely horse. He may have to be put down. He just laid down for four days without moving, the vet gave him injections to ease the pain, he was home though and I would look after him.

The main concern was for Bluey's health, I wasn't interested in racing him again, in fact the vets told me it would be more humane to put him down but I would have none of that. If I could get him back walking and then maybe trotting around his yard that would be OK, he would have a good home for the rest of his life. I treated his legs and gave him lots of TLC. He responded and was up and walking around. I would take him down to the beach every day, swim him and wade him in the water.

He was very well bred and with his great ability he would make a very good stallion. I would breed from him, he would like that. He deserves some of the spoils for having so much courage and being an all round good guy. I purchased some really well bred brood mares, some a bit old that horse studs thought were nearly finished as far as breeding goes. I got some very good mares cheap because of this.

Graeme in Coffs Harbour

I was studying breeding going right back into the NZ and American racing and was become an authority on this. Bluey was thriving, he loved his new life and soon we had lots of new foals. His legs were looking good—this horse was a miracle.

In the off breeding season, I decided that he needed to be kept fit, I started to ride him down at the beach, I'd never been on a horse before on my life, it didn't matter, I had faith in Bluey, he would look after me. I then tried him in the jog cart. I bought some old harnesses and an old jog cart and off we went. I nearly fell out a few times, once again, Bluey was gentle with me. Who was training who I'm not sure. I could tell he really loved this so I took him to the track for a light run, I tried to look like I knew what I was doing, the other trainers must've had a giggle, who cares, we were having fun!

Things were getting serious, Bluey was like his old self. I was still treating his legs and bandaging them every time we went for a run, and I started to dream that he might race again. I knew one thing for sure, he thought he could. I applied for a Trainer's Licence, there was no way I would give him to any other trainer again. Not many trainers believed in beach training in those days, they worked their horses on the hard tracks. I was working Bluey on the sand. I took him to a friend's property in Baldivis. Noel Firken had a big sandy track out in the bush. I would take him there, work him, then go to the beach. He was thriving.

Glen with her horse in 1997

Will I or wont I? Yes I would! I entered him for a race, I could still imagine the comments of the trotting community, "this guy must be mad". He started at long odds in a field which was about five classes below him. He was inspected by the course vet before the race. They didn't want him to break down and cause an accident. He blitzed the field and won easily. His driver said "he was only in second gear". He had another four races and won them all and then I gave him a break. He was back better than ever! Even the leading trainers were coming to me for advice. They would say "we have a horse with similar injuries to your horse, what did you do that worked so well?". I thought "well you've just got ordinary horses, I've got Bluey".

Bluey's foals were now yearlings and I had a paddock full of them. They were eating me out of house and home. Instead of putting them in the yearling sales, I decided to sell them privately. Most trainers want racing stock by imported stallions, nevertheless, there was a lot of interest. I sold most of them at a fairly competitive price but was left with three or four. I decided to train these myself. It was interesting, the ones that sold were the good looking ones whereas the leftovers were the ones I liked. I thought they had the better breeding on the mare's side and somehow I liked the little scruffy ones, they always seemed to try harder.

They were a success when they started racing as early two year olds, which is always a good sign for a new stallion. Some of my horses won some big races, while others were consistent money earners. I could fill the whole book with my 20 years as a horse trainer. I trained the winners of well over 100 races and I'm very proud of this, especially as I started somewhat late in life and not knowing the first thing about training horses. Nearly all my winners I bred myself.

Some of the more prominent ones were Maybe Matilda, she was a WA Oaks winner; Hey I'm Lucky, a great little horse who should have won The Golden Nugget which was a $100,000 race. He suffered severe interference when leading at the start, went back to last and finished a really good fifth. There was Sightseer, who was a very consistent city winner; Hey Hey Jose he was a very good young horse and won lots of races in Perth, I finished up selling him to America. Another horse called Hey What Luck, was injured in a race fall but he had so much ability he could've been my best horse.

Graeme was a great help with the horses and after he went to Coffs Harbour, I employed a stable hand named Kathy Chambers, she was a licensed trainer in her own right. During one period, we were winning races nearly every week in Perth. I featured near the top of the trainers list on winners to starters over this period. This was recognised by my peers because winners to starters is the name of the game. Some trainers would start sometimes a dozen horses every night at Gloucester Park, winning one every now and again.

Racing is probably the toughest way to make a living, you compete against multimillionaires right down to very desperate people. The millionaires spend big money on their horses and give them to the top trainers, while some of the desperate people most times just race to feed their family. Some of these people are dodgy and will do anything to win but overall the majority of owners and trainers are just good people who love horses. I knew of people who had two or three jobs just so they could afford to race a horse. Most times their horses were looked after better than they treated themselves. It didn't seem to matter to some of these people, whether their horse was slow or fast, horses were in their blood.

CHAPTER 17

BYFORD DAYS

A lot happened in our 18 or so years living on the farm at Byford. Some good and some not so good. One of the good ones was Lisa's marriage. We hadn't given up on her but at 33 years of age we were getting a little worried. "I haven't found the right man" she said. She also wanted a family but it would have to be in wedlock. I guess Paul was worth waiting for.

Paul and Lisa on their wedding day

I clearly remember him coming to speak to me one day. I was out in the hayshed making up the feeds for my horses. He said out of the blue "I would like your permission to marry your daughter". It caught me by surprise, not that I didn't think Paul and Lisa wouldn't get married, that seemed fairly obvious, it was just that Lisa wasn't a young kid and he didn't need my permission. In fact I didn't think that sort of thing was still done. I did however, appreciate him asking, it showed his true character. I can remember telling Gaye's dad saying "Gaye and I are getting married" and that was that. She was only 18 and I was 22 and it was in 1961, now it was 1994. Still it was a nice thing for Paul to do.

I went back up to the house with a big smile on my face. Lisa and Gaye said "What's going on?". I said "Nothing, you'll see". Weeks went by and nothing happened. Gaye said "Lisa is worried, she was almost certain Paul was going to ask her to marry him". I thought so too but kept quiet not wanting to complicate matters. The engagement was soon announced and I breathed a sigh of relief. They were married at Lisa's place with the reception being held at a nearby hotel.

Their wedding was a great day, very casual with only close relatives and friends attending. Some family on both sides of the family came from Melbourne and Graeme came from Coffs Harbour. It was great to see him, we hadn't seen him for a few years and he looked good. Lisa's cousin Jan, which is my sister Lea's daughter, came from Melbourne and she was a great help to Lisa. It was good to see Lisa married and Paul was certainly worth waiting for. There didn't seem to be much chance of Graeme getting married, although he said he had a girlfriend in Coffs Harbour, she was a school teacher with a 10 year old daughter. Nothing was to come of this romance.

When Lisa had come back from her overseas trip she bought a nice little house in North Perth. It was unusual in those days for a young, single girl to buy a house on her own. Lisa however, always had her head screwed on right. It turned out to be a great little investment. She had started to renovate it by herself, mainly just decorating but after they were married and Paul moved in they both started some serious renovations. I can remember them all living in the front bedroom as the whole back of the house was completely demolished and rebuilt. My first grandson William had come along by this time and it was a nightmare keeping him out of all the mess as he was just a little toddler.

As I mentioned before, there were also some of the worst times of my life while we were living at the farm. Mum passed away, not unexpectedly as she was well into her nineties and quite frail. She'd only recently moved into a care home. She had been very independent and lived on her own until she was ninety. After Dad passed away, she moved from Rosebud into a unit in Beaumaris. Glen and Lea kept an eye on her. I travelled to Melbourne for the funeral feeling very remorseful. It hit home to me that I'd missed a lot of my parent's life, especially in their final years. It was left up to Lea and Glen to be there for them. Their husbands Keith and Murray were also very much involved.

Graeme and Gaye

It was also lovely to see Mum when Lea and Glen bought her over to see me when we moved into the farm. Mum was a bit frail but well enough to enjoy the trip. It was much appreciated by me.

Helping to make this a dark period of my life was the death of my best mate Ron and Mike on consecutive Christmases.

There was another nasty shock in store, Gaye had been feeling poorly for some time and her doctor was treating her for pneumonia. As part of her treatment she had to have a lung x-ray and the doctor noticed a shadow on one of her lungs and suggested some tests just to make sure. It was devastating news, the tests came back positive as cancer. She was rushed to Sir Charles Gardner Hospital and admitted for further tests. She was to start a course of chemotherapy immediately. The doctor told us not to worry as she was young, only in her 30s, and the cancer was in the early stages. However, we couldn't help thinking at this period in time it was 2.5% survival rate for this type of cancer. We only thought about this, never actually said it of course.

Our life was put on hold. In fact it was turned upside down. Lots of families have been touched by cancer but until it hits you directly it is very hard to describe. We all take it differently. Friends were supportive but not really knowing how to help or what to say. Some just cried. Others chose to just carry on as if nothing had happened. I think Graeme took it worse than anyone, he was very angry and became withdrawn. He was a teenager at this time and it was a difficult enough age as it was. At one stage he started to go off the rails somewhat. I guess we were guilty of losing the plot to some extent.

The chemo was having a terrible effect on Gaye, apparently people have various reactions to some of the chemicals. Gaye couldn't eat during the different periods of treatment. She lost so much weight I could pick her up with one hand. Of course she lost her hair but that was normal. I would make a drink for her every morning made of vegetable and fruit and vitamins. Some days this was the only nourishment she would have for the whole day. I would take the drink into her and have the unpleasant task of waking her up. She wouldn't move of a night while sleeping and lying there she would be the same colour as the bed linen. I would say a prayer when I shook her, with my worst nightmare being that she wouldn't respond.

Once awake she would spend the morning sitting on the bed with all her precious possessions laid out in groups with little notes attached as to who they were to go to. I would say "This isn't necessary, stay positive, you will be OK.", however I would think we should think about making out our wills but I wouldn't mention this to her.

To her credit, in between treatments and when she was feeling reasonable, she would go to work at Alan Linney's shop in the Pioneer Village.

One day after a bad bout of treatment she informed me that she had told the doctors that she wasn't having any more chemo. "That's it, I don't care if I die, enough is enough." They weren't impressed and we later learnt that they had held out little hope for her recovery. They talked her into having radiotherapy on her head as the brain would be the first place the cancer would spread to if it came back. Gaye has been in remission now for nearly 30 years. The cancer and their treatments have taken their toll but it was only really in the last 10 years that her quality of life has suffered. I think the radiotherapy was the main cause in her losing her hearing.

CHAPTER 18

SMOKING

During the early days of Gaye's treatment she was still smoking. Not in front of me of course, but it was obvious she had gone underground. I would find cigarettes in her handbag and I would confiscate them with neither of us saying anything. I became an expert at finding her other hideaways as well, the biscuit barrel, on ledges outside, I was awake up to it all.

To her credit, she was trying to kick the habit and was on all sorts of treatments. One I can remember was that she would listen to tapes of waves and softly speaking people about things that I couldn't understand, a type of brainwashing I suppose. She would have earplugs in day and night. Something worked as she finally beat it. I am of the belief that you can't really give up an addiction unless deep down inside you've had enough. You just beat it yourself.

I was a weekend smoker at one stage of my life. A packet of cigarettes would last me a whole week but I might smoke them all on one or two nights. If I was with my mates at a BBQ and having a couple of beers the whole packet would go. Once night we were playing cards at Val and Mal's place, Judy and Phil were also there. It lasted until the early hours, a great night but the next day I was as sick as a dog. Something had to give. It came down to the smokes or drink.

I have never been a heavy drinker but I did enjoy a beer sometimes with friends on the weekend so it was the smokes that had to go. I vowed never to have another cigarette again for the rest of my life. I psyched myself into this, I told myself I would be violently ill if I even had one cigarette. It worked and I am the worst case now of the reformed smoker you could imagine. Sometimes having to stop myself from lecturing people on it's evils. I guess you have to hit rock bottom and that morning after was my rock bottom. I think this is the way it works with other drugs, they reach rock bottom and with nowhere else to go, hopefully they can give it up and kick it.

Graeme smoked and I could never understand this. He knew it was bad and it nearly killed his mother but I guess he liked it and wasn't ready to give it up. Am I strong willed or just lucky or just kidding myself? I don't know but of course I'm not the first or the last person to give up smoking I just think I am.

In Gaye's case, she started smoking at an early age. Not sure how early, but I can remember her at the age of about 14 puffing away in the kitchen of her home. I would think "this kid needs a good hiding". I think most of her family smoked at that time and her mother died from a cigarette related illness but then again, so did my father.

CHAPTER 19

GOODBYE HORSES

The neighbours were subdividing their properties so I went along with them. I didn't need so much acreage now as I didn't have so many horses on the property. At the height of Bluey's stud career, I had as many as 50 horses to look after. Half of these were mares sent to Bluey, the other half were my own horses. I was scaling down Bluey's stud duties, he had gone blind in one eye when he'd knocked his head in his stable somewhere but apart from that he was in tiptop condition. Later on, maybe two years or so, he went completely blind. I wasn't aware of this at first, he would trot around his paddock coming over to the fence when I came by so we could have a little chat. It was only when I shifted his feed bin to another location that I realised something was wrong. He couldn't find his bin. He could still service mares but I would only use him on a couple of my own mares. He still knew me of course and I put a pony in with him for company and he seemed happy.

The property was divided into five acre lots and this suited me as we were now more or less just a racing stable. The horses were doing well and I built some new stables and landscaped my now much smaller property. I now had a new stable hand Kathy Chambers. She was a licenced trainer in her own right and an expert horsewoman. We were a good team, taking the horses to the beach and fast working them together on the Byford track. Graeme was still in Coffs Harbour at this stage so Kathy was very valuable.

Gaye was fit and well but we were drifting apart. Our friends first noticed this and eventually they persuaded Gaye to move out and try living by herself for a while. She moved to a home unit in Alfred Cove. She knew this suburb really well from the old days.

Graeme came back and was helping me with the horses but the writing was on the wall, we would eventually have to sell the property and Gaye and I would go our separate ways. No property meant no horses. Graeme and I decided we needed to plan ahead. We would work and race the horses until the property was sold and then we would look around for a business.

We both liked the idea of a fish and chip shop. We had always thought we could do a better job of cooking fish and chips than other shops. I had done my homework and was checking out shops of a night to see how busy they were. A shop in Mill Point Road, South Perth was for sale, it was in an ideal location and was quite busy so we bought it. During the day we raced horses and of a night we were in the food business.

The property sold and I moved to South Perth. I had sold my horses one by one over the previous six months and a friend and neighbour said they would give Bluey a good home. This was a real load off my mind.

The shop at first went well but we discovered the turnover figures presented to us were nowhere near what they were meant to be. This apparently is quite normal in this sort of business. Graeme was worried. We had spent a lot of money upgrading the product, buying top quality fresh fish and changing the cooking oil from beef tallow to top grade Canola Oil. This was against all advice, everyone said it wouldn't taste the same as your traditional fish and chips. Also we changed the batter to a much lighter one and also introduced a large range of fresh salads. Graeme was in charge of filleting the fish and cooking it in the fryers. I was to do grilled fish and co-ordinate the running of the shop.

The product was healthy, well, as healthy as fish and chips could be I suppose, and top quality and soon the customers came, in fact they came in droves. This part of South Perth had a very dense population and we soon found out they didn't like to cook their own meals. It was scary some nights as the shop would fill up and we would have phone orders and hungry customers. We were still feeling our way and trying new systems to improve our service. The best advertising of course is word of mouth and the word had got out. The fryers were very old and would break down regularly, usually at our busiest time, there would be panic, I soon learnt to stay focussed on the job at hand, never look at a shop full of hungry customers, all trying to catch your eye. Melinda, the cashier, was the only one allowed to converse with the hoards. Everyone else was to just do their job. On the weekends we would have up to seven staff on hand.

Graeme and I in our South Perth shop.

I can remember one night we were packed out and the dockets which had all the orders on them fell into one of the fryers, we fished it out but it was almost impossible to decipher them. About 20 people had to be called up one by one to repeat their order. Each time they would think their order was filled and confusion really reigned that night. But the product in food shops is what you live and die on, customers will come back if they like what you serve them. If you have every watched the sitcom Seinfeld, and the soup Nazi episode you will know exactly what I mean. We were friendly though, not like the soup Nazi. Just a little scared at first but as with any other job, we grew into it and soon got on top of things.

Gaye and I were now living completely separate lives. Graeme and I were living and working in South Perth and Gaye was living her own life in Alfred Cove. She was however, having some problems. First she had a car accident, hitting a young teenager on a bicycle, he had crossed in front of her against the traffic lights and didn't have a light on his bike. It was dark and the Leach Highway wasn't well lit. They boy was badly injured but recovered. Gaye wasn't charged over the accident. No sooner had she got her car back from the repair shop, she had another accident in Armadale. She drove through a stop sign and hit a car, no-one was injured. She wasn't charged over this accident either as the stop sign had been down for some reason, maybe under repair. Still it was a worry and I wasn't sure if she should be driving or whether it was just bad luck. This all happened in 1996 and she is still driving now without any more accidents but her driving is a bit of a worry.

CHAPTER 20

MARGARET RIVER

Lea and Keith came over to visit from over East. I took a couple of days off and we all went down to Margaret River. It was a good break as I had been working hard. I noticed an empty shop in the main street and thought it would be a great location for a seafood cafe restaurant. I had a vision, in fact, it had been on my mind for some time. A customer in South Perth had come to me with a proposal, her young daughter was my phone order girl, which is beside the point I suppose, anyway, she had proposed that she buy my shop and the one next door and turn them into a super seafood restaurant. We would be partners and I would run the restaurant.

The shop next door was on a corner and owned by the same person as mine. The shops were old and had been in the family for over 40 years, this lady, I forget her name, had the buildings valued and put the proposition to the owners. They agreed but at about ten times the market value. I was disappointed, I would've loved to operate on this scale. We had the customers, but could hardly handle them in our old shop. If I sold South Perth and relocated to Margaret River, I could build my dream restaurant. I would have no trouble selling South Perth and let's face it, Margaret River was an idyllic location. It was the place to be.

Before driving back to Perth I had started negotiations to buy the Margaret River shop. It had been a jewellery store and they had relocated further into the main street to a smaller shop. There would have to be massive changes to change an ex-jewellery shop into a restaurant but I was up for it. I soon found a buyer for South Perth but the owners were playing hard ball, my three year lease was up and they wouldn't renew it, they obviously wanted the shop back. Their family had been in the fish and chip business all their lives, I had built the business up and trebled the turnover. I engaged a lawyer and threatened to sue under the Unfair Trade Practices Act, they gave in without a whimper and I was on my way to Margaret River.

Murray and I check out the Charlie's specials, in Margaret River

Charlie's Seafood Restaurant in Margaret River

I employed a local builder and we set about converting the shop. It was a mammoth exercise, lots of stainless steel, new gas fryers, refrigerated display counters, I found someone in Perth whose restaurant was closing, he had a whole truckload of goodies—tables, chairs, fridges, freezers, plates, cutlery, coffee machine, the whole lot, so I bought it all. It was already on the truck so he delivered it to Margaret River for me. I was still living in South Perth and would come down south every two weeks. It was slow going. I needed permits for just about everything and the Shire had a reputation for being hard to get along with. Still, it all came together and we opened in a blaze of glory.

I had hired local staff which turned out to be a mistake. They didn't need much encouragement to go surfing and forget about work. The shop was very busy and the locals loved the product. I hired a chef, she had done four years of her course so she considered herself a chef. We had some great dishes on our menu, all seafood, however I was to learn a thing or two about Margaret River.

For about four months during the winter, there were little or no tourists which meant I had to rely on the locals. They were loyal but no-one eats fish and chips every day and I found out that this wasn't South Perth who had an endless population. Summer was good, the town was packed and we would be flat out. However, I would need a large team to handle it. I had always paid good wages and looked after my staff. Most of the busy trading income was going on paying wages. It also didn't help that some staff like to go on holidays at the busiest times or just simply resign. Loyalty—there was none!!

I soon learnt backpackers were the way to go. There were heaps of them in town and no-one seemed to want to employ them. I would just ask them to level with me, if their Visa was still current and they could give me three months guaranteed work I would put them on. It worked, they all seemed to need money. The locals would quite often work only until they had enough to catch up on their rent and have a bit extra to party with. Then they would go on a surfing and party bender for a few weeks.

Graeme didn't come to Margaret River with me so I was doing it all alone and after three years of seven days a week I was getting worn out. Plus, I wasn't making a fortune, more or less working flat out to just pay the rent and the staff. I was losing interest and when this happens to a business it goes south very quickly. Graeme came down from Perth to help me. It was great to have some support.

One of the first things Graeme said to me was "What's wrong with you?". "What do you mean?" I asked. "You look so old" he replied. "I am old" I said. I was in my sixties now but Graeme said I looked much older. When Graeme and I work together it is a love/hate relationship. We squabble a lot over details. He wants to do things his way and I want to do things my way. We usually agree on the big picture however.

He was hopeless at organising things and administration, I was good at this and he was good at the hands on work, both with horses and cooking, it all had to be done just right which is good of course except that he wasn't very tolerant with staff. "If we are paying them good money" he would say "they must shape up". I would agree but I was forever being the diplomat, patching up disputes with a disgruntled workforce. He would say "just get rid of them, I'll do it all myself". Anyway, we were fighting which wasn't unusual. One day he said "you should go and see a Doctor and get some anti-depressants". "Why would I do that?" I said. "Because you have a classic case of depression" he told me. Was he right? Is this what's wrong with me? "No" I said "I'm not taking any darned anti-depressants, I'm just a bit tired and cranky".

However, I had thought for some time that something more serious was wrong with me. I was waking up some mornings at 3 or 4 am with chest pains. I was secretly worried but like most men I thought it would all go away. I was getting home from the shop at about 10 pm, I would have a beer, usually about one to relax me, then I would cook something for dinner. I was normally very hungry, most times I hadn't eaten since breakfast. It was just indigestion I thought. One morning at about 3 am the pain was so bad I just sat up in bed and

waited until 8 am, got dressed and went to see my doctor. He sent me
to the hospital for an ECG and numerous other tests. Then back to the
doctor for the results, where he said "I wish I had a heart as good as
yours". "Well, what's wrong with me?" I asked. "If my heart's OK just
give me some pills, painkillers, anti-depressants, whatever". "You don't
need antidepressants" he said "you just need to change your lifestyle,
take a holiday". "Great idea" I replied, "who will run my business,
maybe I'll just close up for a few weeks, it's not that easy. It's OK for
you, you just get in a locum if you want a holiday, get someone else to
take over." He just said "it's your life, see you later". "What about the
pain?" I asked. He said "if I give you pain relief, you will just continue
on your way and then one day you will just drop dead".

I realised I hadn't had a holiday for over 25 years. He was probably
right. Graeme said "Let's get out of here, sell up and let's move on". I
found out that more than half the cafes and restaurants in Margaret
River were for sale. Rents in the main street were overinflated. Too
many eating houses and not enough customers was everyone's problem,
not only mine. Even today, rents in the main street are crippling
businesses even though Margaret River's population has increased
dramatically. The business broker said "you have a very nice shop but
with so many businesses for sale it could take a while to sell". Graeme
said "what if we give it three months? If we don't sell by then, we
walk". I reluctantly agreed.

We did find a buyer, not at the price we wanted. I had already put
it on the market at a competitive price, way under what it had cost me
originally to set up. Still, buyers were scarce and they had plenty to
choose from. I accepted the offer but the buyer kept playing games.
It started with the microwave, could I take it off the price, he had
his own mircrowave? OK, it was only a microwave and I could use
it myself. Then there was the fryer, he wasn't going to have a seafood
restaurant, he was going to cook Polish food, "that would go over
really well in Margaret River I thought"!! Then he didn't want one of
the display fridges or the cooking range, it was a nice new stove and
oven but I thought maybe Lisa could do with it she was renovating her

kitchen. It was getting out of hand, what would I do with 60 dinner plates? I told the agent to send him packing. At this rate I would owe him money. He agreed it wasn't ethical and he had signed the offer of acceptance, still, we were a long way down the track with the sale so I stuck with it.

I can remember the day of the handover, I had hired a big trailer and Graeme and I were dismantling half the shop and loading it onto the trailer, we were having difficulty getting our giant menu board down when the buyer walked in. It was another item he didn't want, it had cost me about $2,000 to have made and I had offered it to him at half that price. He didn't need it he said, "just take it off the sale price", that's another $2,000 off. As we were struggling to take it down he suggested that it might be easier to leave it there, "what can you do with it anyway?". He said he'd give me $200 for it right here and now if you like. I said "no, its not for sale at any price, I have a use for it". We took it to Augusta to our new house and there it stayed in our shed for nearly 10 years, I wasn't going to give him the satisfaction, I was sick of playing his games, it might be the way they did things in Poland but I do business with a handshake and stick to the deal. That's the Aussie way. Polish food, is he for real? He lasted for about six months and the business changed hands again. Did he go broke? Do you think I care? Sure did, I hope so!! Call it sour grapes if you like. I drive past that shop nearly every week, but like all my other projects I have no regrets, you move on, no good going back in time unless you are thinking of the good times.

We thought about going back to Perth but quickly dismissed this idea, we had visited Augusta a few times, mainly to make contact with fishermen and we loved the place. Most residents of Margaret River will tell you Augusta is the end of the earth, dull, boring, nothing happens there. They're right of course!! It is the end of the earth the most south west part of Australia that you can go to, the next stop is the South Pole. As for dull and boring, maybe, but that was exactly what I needed.

I rented a house right on the Blackwood River in Victoria Parade. I could walk across the road, throw a line in and catch fish, how good would that be? Also, there was a boat ramp almost opposite the house. Both Graeme and I love fishing, Graeme, being better at it than me. I lack patience and maybe a bit of skill. The house had a big, new shed at the back where we stored the equipment from the shop. There was enough room left over for three or four cars. Also out the back was a self-contained granny flat and Graeme could live in that and I would have the house to myself.

After a busy day moving, we settled down to spend our first night in Augusta. We were sitting out on the front porch having a well earned beer, we couldn't believe how quiet it was. It was just on dusk and rabbits were appearing from nowhere. Tom, our blue heeler, was in his element, chasing them all over the place. He also like chasing seagulls, never caught any but it wasn't for lack of trying.

The stillness of the night was broken by an unusual sound coming from the river. There was a flock of pelicans just opposite but it wasn't them. Soon a pod of dolphins appeared swimming and playing on their way up the river. How good was this??? It turned out they would come up the river twice a day. Once when we were out in our boat at the mouth of the river, they circled our boat, Graeme dived overboard and swam with them for quite some time. It was unreal!!

On this subject, a couple of years later while fishing out in the bay, the whale watching boat was nearby. A whale surfaced right next to our boat. I could've touched it with my fishing rod. It had a look at us and then disappeared under the boat coming up on the other side some 50 metres away. It didn't even cause a ripple or rock our little boat. It then let off a blast of air. It was an amazing experience.

I suggested to Graeme that we sleep in the day after our move, never, ever, done that before in my life except maybe the odd day when I might have been sick. I had no commitments also probably for the first time in my life. I wanted have a coffee at that nice little cafe in town, let someone else wait on us for a change. Graeme wanted to look around for a boat and catch up with some of the fishermen he had made friends with and get a job. Fishing would be a job he'd love, anything to do with animals and the ocean were Graeme's passion.

Graeme Surfing

CHAPTER 21

RETIREMENT

I hadn't realised it, but I was now officially retired and enjoying it. We'd bought a small boat and we were doing lots of fishing. We'd motor up the Blackwood River catching Black Bream and crabs. We could also catch them just opposite the house. The boat was also big enough to go out into the bay where we would catch all sorts of fish, mainly Pink Snapper, King George Whiting and Skippy. We had a couple of crayfish pots and when we got lucky, crayfish was on the menu. If the weather was rough we could always walk across the road and catch whiting. Graeme would sometimes get up at about 4 or 5 in the morning and go down to the town jetty. He would always come home with fish.

We also played golf some days at the little nine hole golf course. We thought about joining the golf club at the main course but somehow we never got around to it. Graeme had a job now with a fisherman. This was scary as they would go out for days, right out into the deep water off Augusta, fishing for King Crabs. The owner of the boat had a reputation for treating his deckhands badly—lots of hard work and not much pay. Not feeding them very well when they were out at sea and just ignoring basic safety issues. I was glad when he left and joined another boat. When the weather was bad he had a part time job at the caravan park doing maintenance. He also looked after a disabled boy two days a week, taking him to Margaret River for physio treatment. He went to Bunbury for a few days to complete a first aid course also. His experience with Zack, the disabled boy, plus his first aid certificates helped him to later on land a good job at the local Augusta hospital.

Despite enjoying the easy life in Augusta I wasn't happy. I would have bad dreams like I was a stranger, just lost, an outsider. My friends seemed to be talking together in these dreams and I would always be looking in but not being part of the discussion. No-one seemed to want to know me. This would carry over into the day. Why didn't anyone like me anymore? I knew the answer, I was a loser! I had failed in Margaret River, I had let everyone down. It was the first time in my life I had failed at anything or so I thought. Sure my marriage wasn't perfect and it was hard at times when I was training horses a feast when winners came easy and a famine when nothing went right. Horses breaking down, bad luck, all sorts of things happen. Racing was without doubt the hardest way to make a living, yet I had succeeded to some extent anyway. I was a good aircraft engineer, I was a very respected jeweller and my shop in South Perth was rated in the best fish and chip shops in Perth so why am I a failure?

Yes, its official! I have Depression. If I didn't have it before, I certainly have it now! It was all adding up. Before Graeme came down to help me at Charlie's Seafood Cafe in Margaret River, I had dreams of buying a campervan and travelling around Australia, getting away from that fantastic shop I had built up from nothing. I don't think this was unusual, lots of people want to do this but another thought I had when things got really bad was to just buy a tent and go bush. There were people on the outskirts of Margaret River who lived like this. Hippies we used to call them, now it is known as an "alternate lifestyle". Now as ridiculous as this idea sounds now, I was seriously considering it. I was in a bad place mentally and it was only now that I was really coming to terms with it. The doctor was right, change my lifestyle or perish. That was OK for the physical side, my body was better, no more chest pains, but my head was still far from right. Doing nothing wasn't the answer, neither were antidepressants, I wasn't going down that path. I needed to get some purpose back in my life.

I could join the local football club. I'm sure I could help on the administration side, after all I have had 30 years experience with the Victoria Park Football Club. Another option was the bowling club.

Friends recommended that this was a great pastime. I was a little hesitant however, I knew I would get too competitive. I suffered a little from whiteline fever when playing football. Not as bad as Hayden Ballantyne but I guess I did have a little bit of him in me. I could just see me taking to some old guy who I thought wasn't taking it seriously enough and letting the side down. Even when Graeme and I would play golf it sometimes ended up in a squabble over the scores. That's how competitive we were.

The Lions Club was an option, they did a great job in Augusta and I did have some association with them helping with their recycling at one stage. A job would be good, I was still young enough to work and the thought of living out my life on the pension worried me. I could get a part time job with the local fish and chip shop. Graeme had worked on and off in that shop and I knew the work back to front. I would enjoy it, although I knew I would try and tell him how to run his business. Graeme had made lots of suggestions to him while he was working there but I think it went right over the top of the guy's head.

First though I would have to get myself fit, my left knee was giving me trouble, I'd had a complete knee joint replacement in my right knee some years ago, this was the knee I'd hurt playing football when I was young. Now my left knee was a mess. Years of horse training and standing on it in the shops had taken their toll. I went to Perth to see my surgeon and he put me into hospital the next day for another completely new knee joint. This operation isn't for the faint hearted but after the rehab the benefits far outweigh the trauma, as long as you put the work into strengthening the leg.

Gaye drove me back to Augusta where she dropped a bombshell. She had invested all her life savings with a dodgy finance broker. He was a crook who fleeced hundreds of vulnerable people and finished up doing ten years in jail. Graeme Grubb was his name and with a name like that it should've set off alarm bells. It would've with me! Still, all her money was gone and there was nothing we could do about it. We talked it over and came to the conclusion that the best thing for her to do was to move to Augusta.

When my knee was strong enough, I started to look around for work. I took over the distribution co-ordination for the South West Times and other advertising material. I could do this from home and hired people to do the actual deliveries. I wouldn't make megabucks but it would give me independence and maybe I could put a bit aside so I could travel. I'd always loved travelling and that would be good for my wellbeing.

I also took on some community volunteer work at the local hospital, Meals on Wheels and driving patients to Margaret River and Busselton for specialist treatments. I was feeling better. The bad dreams had gone and I was back to my old positive self. No longer a loser!! Graeme said that I was never a loser, I had let no-one down, only myself. I had hurt no-one except myself. You have to prove this to yourself however.

CHAPTER 22

TURKEY TRIP

After some years in our Victoria Parade house we were offered a unit in the Leeuwin Units near the Hospital. This had lots of advantages, it was a nice little community and financially we would be better off. As it was near the hospital, nurses and orderlies were on hand to assist anyone who required it, this was another advantage. So we shifted house. We didn't want to leave our house by the river and the landlords didn't want to see us go. They'd given us virtually all the help we'd needed and we had treated it like our own house and they appreciated that, but times change so we moved. It meant Graeme would have to find his own accommodation. This would be a blessing in disguise as it was about time he moved out, let him fend for himself. He had plenty of friends in Augusta so there were plenty of options for him.

The year was 2008 and after a couple of years in the unit I was getting bored. Cooped up in a small place with Gaye meant we were certain to get on each other's nerves. I had to get away, a trip seemed like the answer. Lea and Keith had talked about the wonderful time they had in Turkey. It sounded good to me. I had travelled to most of the other countries that regular travellers go to. Turkey would be exciting. Friends didn't think it was a good idea and asked me if I'd ever seen the movie Midnight Express. I had, but I didn't intend to smuggle drugs so I couldn't see their point. I would join a travel group, it would be more fun that way. Gaye didn't want to go and I guess she wasn't really up to it anyway. I would go in April so I could be in Gallipoli on ANZAC Day.

The tour group comprised of 38 of us, predominantly American with five Aussies, four Kiwis and a few Canadians. It was exciting, I loved

Turkey. We were to spend 14 days touring mainly West and Central Turkey. The East was a bit dicey with borders on Iraq, Iran and Syria so we wouldn't go there. The Turkey I saw was very safe, mainly Islamic but certainly very friendly. We were to end the trip at Gallipoli before returning to Istanbul. The Americans didn't have a clue why we were there at Gallipoli but I soon put them straight, along with a bit of help from two Kiwis, Dave and Merryn. These two were good companions on the trip and we still communicate regularly, they are lovely people.

Talking to Richard on the Turkey trip.
Dick in the foreground with the cane

The Turkish Tour Guide had a similar view on what Gallipoli was all about as I had. I admired him for this. The Turkish people respect our ANZACs, I'm not sure I would have if the boot was on the other foot and they were trying to invade us. I met another person on the trip who I spent a bit of time with, an American woman called Katherine, she had travelled to most countries but not Australia. She wanted to know all about Australia. I told her first you have to talk like an Aussie, no more "oh my God", you need to replace this with "crikey". She was getting good at it and connecting with my sense of humour.

Once outside a mosque, the third for the day, the tour director asked if there were any questions, Katherine piped up saying "When are we going to see some decent tucker on this tour?". The guide said without missing a beat "tomorrow, you will see some I'm sure". The Americans were talking amongst themselves saying "tomorrow, the mosques have some good tucker, that'll be exciting". I smiled, I had taught her well. Even today she keeps an Aussie slang book next to her TV just in case an Aussie program comes on so she can tell what we're talking about. She got the DVD Gallipoli when she returned home from the tour, even though she despised Mel Gibson, but she enjoyed the movie.

Another interesting character on this tour was a man from Sydney called Richard. He was much the same age as me and he was my tour bus companion. Richard was good company and a bit like the character Felix from The Odd Couple. I guess I was the other half of that couple and we had some fun times. Another guy, Dick, was an elderly American who also made us laugh. He called me "his little Aussie pal" and was one of the few Americans who was awake up to my sense of humour. I'd learnt a few words of Turkish before coming on the tour and one day whilst waiting to board our bus, we were outside on a busy street and a group of school boys came past. They saw my Aussie cap with a kangaroo on it and started talking to me. I conversed with them in my limited Turkish and they were talking back to me with their school English. Neither the boys nor myself had a clue what we were saying but it looked like we were having a great conversation. The tour group were spellbound, they couldn't believe I could speak fluent Turkish. Dick was onto me however, and he laughed saying that I was full of bullshit! He was probably right. Another person I was friendly with was a woman from Palm Springs called Norma. We still communicate sometimes on Facebook.

I spent five days in Istanbul by myself after the tour and mixed with the locals. It was fun. I was back to my old self and was already planning my next trip. Other good news was that Gaye was getting some of her money back, even though he was a crook, Graeme Grubb had made some good investments and the receivers were selling them off at a good price.

Phil and I at my 70th Party

Friends and Family at my 70th party

CHAPTER 23

TRAGEDY

Life was fairly full at this time, first was a trip to Melbourne for a family reunion, a Christmas Day lunch at Gavin and Rene's home. Gavin is sister Glen's son and brother to Tracey. Gaye and I stayed at Glen and Murray's lovely home at Mt Martha. It was great that Graeme came also and he stayed at his cousin Neal's home in East Preston. Neal is sister Lea's son.

The day was a great success with a large gathering of family and friends. We came bearing gifts. Lisa couldn't make it so she sent some wine with us. Gaye had made a huge Christmas cake. We stayed for a few more days with Glen and Murray after Christmas Day. This was great, I'd stayed there before and had always had a lovely time.

Next was my 70th birthday, Lisa was going to give me a party at her place in City Beach. Lots of old friends attended and I was very grateful to all the family who had travelled from over East. Mim and Tony, old friends from America were surprise visitors which was great as we hadn't seen them for a while. Lea and Keith, their daughter Michelle and son Neal came down to Augusta for a few days. This was much appreciated. We went to lunch at a Margaret River winery called Voyager. I had been given a voucher as a birthday present and it was a real pleasure to host this lunch.

At this time, something happened that was unbelievable, something that I'm going to have trouble talking about. I lost my son and best friend Graeme. He passed away at the too young age of 45. These things aren't supposed to happen and it hit me very hard. We are still not too sure exactly how or why but he just went to sleep and didn't wake up.

This period of his life was more than likely his best period. He had been employed by the Augusta Hospital and loved his job. The staff and patients also loved him. He was first employed as an orderly but was doing a course to be upgraded to a carer. His kind nature made this a perfect job for him. One of the nurses was very keen on him and maybe at last he might have settled into a steady relationship. Graeme always loved kids but he had told me on numerous occasions that he didn't want to get into a serious relationship as he had nothing much to offer anyone. With his job at the hospital he now had plenty to offer.

Graeme suffered from asthma and he had just changed doctors and his new doctor had changed his medication. It was a Saturday night and Graeme had just finished his shift at the hospital. He came in around 9pm to pick up his puppy Mitzy who I would look after when he went to work. He then went to the pub for a couple of beers with his mates, a thing he did every Saturday night. His housemates said he came home fairly early, in good spirits and went straight to bed as he had a shift at the hospital the next morning. Whether the medication and the mix of alcohol was the cause we don't know, but it seems likely.

We gave him a great funeral. Family came from everywhere, just about the whole town of Augusta attended and the hospital staff were devastated. In the short time he'd worked there which was only about 18 months he was very much loved. We have sprinkled his ashes in the Blackwood River, this is where he would've liked to spend his days. I took ownership of his little dog. Lisa and I had given him the puppy for his birthday only a couple of months before. He had lost his old mate Tom a few weeks earlier. We're not sure how Tom died, I think it was just old age, he was a much loved Blue Heeler and a real town dog. I still have Mitzy. I promised myself I would look after her even though I had plenty of offers to adopt her at the time. She is without doubt my best mate.

Graeme and I had talked about going on a trip around Australia. He had some holidays coming up and this would've been great. We had gone on an outback trip when he was about 10, I'd bought a little Suzuki 4WD and loaded it up with camping gear. We toured around the Murchison area camping out, it was a great father/son bonding exercise. He'd always wanted to go shooting so we went out one night spotlight shooting for rabbits or whatever, maybe a fox and he did shoot a fox from some distance away and when we went up to inspect him, he wasn't dead. I told Graeme that he had to put him out of his distress. Graeme said "No, you do it.". "You must do it" I said "he is your responsibility". He had tears in his eyes and I'm sure his future shooting would be at targets and not at animals.

I had done some research on what sort of vehicle would be best for the trip. I found a 4WD wagon in Melbourne on the internet so I bought it. It would need some modifications and when it was ready I would fly to Melbourne and drive it back but plans were now up in the air. Without Graeme what would be the point? After a few weeks thinking about it I decided I would go ahead, it would do me good to get away and spend some time by myself. I think it was the way Graeme would've wanted it.

CHAPTER 24

TRAVEL DIARY

Day one was off to Kalgoorlie, I was singing along to Blondie and my 60s rock and roll CDs. One benefit of travelling alone was my singing. It's for my ears only. I was also tuning into the truckies with my CB radio, which was fun. I had heaps of navigational gear as I was going right across the middle of central Australia and I had a satellite phone which is a must and a lot of recovery gear. I stopped to have lunch at Southern Cross, a nice little town. This is where I had stayed overnight when I first drove West nearly 50 years ago. Then it was off to Leonora and then the real thing, 450 kms of dirt road to Tjukayirla Roadhouse. It wasn't a bad road, rough in some patches and I was glad I had new tyres. Lots of work was being done on this road but I could average 80 kms per hour safely.

The countryside was a big surprise, no sign of desert yet, lots of green grass, trees and small hills. The soil is red and rich, all it needs is water. It's raining at present only lightly though, just enough to settle the dust. Lots of eagles, camels and wild goats. Next I was off to Warburton and I had programmed Johnny Cash to have his turn on the CDs. Just Johnny and me, I can't wait. On this road I made friends with some bikers, I seem to attract these types. They were travelling from Albany to Darwin and were camping out in tents, it was still raining and there was no chance that I'd put them up in my luxury digs which at this stage was a donga (a shipping container with a bit of furniture in it).

What a difference a day makes, I'm on the road from hell!! 260 kms of corrugations you would lose a small bus in. Lots of bits and pieces of cars on the road and the roadside is littered with wrecks. Thinking I'm going to be the next statistic in the middle of nowhere. The VHF radio antenna has broken off, thank goodness for electrical tape, it fixes everything. The radio still works which is good.

I stopped by what I thought was a circus troope, kids doing cartwheels in the middle of the road, it was an aboriginal family who'd broken down. They didn't seem too concerned though. Even with a broken windscreen, steam coming out of their radiator and a flat battery. They only had 200 kms to go so I guess they had no worries. I gave them a container of water as they had none. The cops were travelling behind me so I left it in their hands. I'd just had breakfast with the cops and I knew it would be safe to stop as they had left just after me. It is advisable not to stop for a group of broken down people they could've just all bundled into my car and I would've had no way of stopping them.

I then arrived at the Warburton Aboriginal Settlement and stayed the night. It's just a donga but it had a shower. Day eight and I was in heaven, the road had just been graded and it's really smooth going. I've been travelling for eight days now and I'm still in the state of Western Australia, tomorrow I cross the border into the Northern Territory and Ayres Rock, Uluru as it is now known.

I'm in spacious quarters at Warakurna and I've also got TV so I'll be able to watch the footy. I'm not sure what time it is, it's central Australian time here which is 1.5 hrs ahead of Western time. The bikies are still tagging along although one has gone missing. I feel safe with them camped outside my door. They're very friendly and I don't think I'd get any intruders with bikies on my doorstep. No communications with the outside world for days, tonight I hope to get through to Lisa or Paul on my satellite phone.

It was a good road to Ayres Rock with lots of roadworks, lots of dingos, camels, birds and other wildlife. The scenery at Docker River on the WA and Northern Territory border was spectacular. The Petermann Ranges make a vast contrast to the flat land which I'd been travelling over. The Olgas and Ayres Rock come into view about

50kms out of Yulara and they are truly amazing. Photos don't do them justice.

I rang Gaye and found out that Mitzy is missing me. There are big plans when I get back. Mitzy and I are moving into a cottage owned by Lisa and Paul. Mitzy is still under a ban from where we live now. We're on the trip from Ayres Rock to Alice Springs which is 500 kms. I'm feeling good now but had a mini meltdown on the way. I was thinking about how good it would've been to have Graeme on the trip and I had to stop and have a walk to get my head together. I thought these feelings were over and done with. I was very tired and maybe that didn't help but I feel good now. I carried Graeme's photo with me and I'm quite comfortable with his death but maybe not as comfortable as I thought I was.

Alice Springs is a lovely town situated right in the centre of Australia, lots of character but very modern. Big granite boulders on the verges make a big change from the dusty landscape I have been travelling through. It seems like half the population is aboriginal. Lots of desert aborigines come into town and with the overnight temperatures dropping to zero you feel sorry for them. There's lots of modern housing and I think most aborigines have jobs. There's plenty of help in town for them—education and health, etc. My UHF radio antenna was repaired and I'm getting ready for the next desert trip through to Queensland.

First stop after the Alice is a camping ground and roadhouse called Gemtree, as the name implies it is gemstone country and lots of tourists from Alice Springs are here as its the weekend, so about 30 caravans are staying the night. Everyone would be fossicking for gems I would imagine, garnets and zircons. The power goes off at 10 pm which means the heater goes off. I woke up at 2am very cold, below zero I was told in the morning. I'm not used to the cold so I got dressed and went back to bed. I had two doonas and two blankets on the bed and I swear ice was forming on the walls. I would've been better sleeping in the van, it would've been warmer. Still, Gemtree was a nice place. The next day I'm off to Jervois, a cattle station that sells fuel, I'll stay overnight and prepare for the worst of the journey, 500 kms of bad road with no stops, no nothing until I get to Boulia a small outback Queensland town and bitumen.

Today's road was very rough and I only came across one vehicle on the road all day, apart from me of course. The scenery was good on this leg, the MacDonnell and Hart's Ranges make for good viewing. I wouldn't like to travel this road in the wet season however, as there are lots of creeks and washaways. I must get up early in the morning, 500 kms of road could take me eight hours or more as I won't be speeding.

I rang home on the satellite phone and Gaye is sick. This is a real worry with me stuck in the middle of nowhere, I just feel so helpless, Lisa has rung the Augusta Hospital and they have sent an orderly over with a wheelchair. She had a good check-up and hopefully all will be well. Lisa is a great help.

I was up at 4.30 am and hit the road at 5 am, it's very dark and cold but the new driving lights on the wagon work really well. It's important to be careful of kangaroos as this is the time of the day that's most dangerous. Kangaroos jump out in front of you, attracted to the headlights, if one finishes up in the front seat kicking and scratching it's not good news. Wreck your car out here and you'd had to hitch your way back home as the trip would be over. The sunrise is spectacular but driving into it no fun. I just missed a kangaroo, he came out of nowhere, jumped out in front of me and put his nose on the bullbar, did a brilliant u-turn and headed back into the bush. If it'd been dark he would've kept going right in front of me.

The road is not as bad as everyone says, the workers are doing a good job. I'm in Queensland now and I drive into Boulia, the first sign of civilisation. Boulia is a nice, friendly town and I'm soon on my way to Winton on the smooth black stuff, narrow with lots of creek crossings but it's smooth. This is channel country where all the rains in North Queensland flow through these plains on their way to Lake Eyre. The flood plain is over three times the size of England and thank goodness it's the dry season, there are creeks and washaways every couple of kms.

This is by far the best and most pleasant and easy part of the trip, lovely green waist high grass and trees. Cattle country and there are plenty of them. The bird life is unbelievable, everything from finches, budgies, swallows, cockatoos, galahs, large water birds, hawks and eagles. Then bang out of the blue I hit an eagle, he was feeding on the roadkill and took off in front of me, lucky I had slowed down as there is nothing more scary than having an eagle sitting on your bonnet staring at you through the windscreen. He hopped off and sat on the roadside with a stunned look on his face, as eagles sometimes do. My football team of choice is the West Coast Eagles and they stand around with stunned looks on their faces quite often. He hopped off before I could get the camera out. Incredibly, there was no damage to the wagon. Some five minutes later I hit a flock of budgies, feathers everywhere, not sure how many survivors there would've been.

I'm now in Winton which is a town with rich history, dinosaur country. More dinosaur fossils found here than anywhere else in the world. As I drive in to town I think "well here comes another old fossil to add to their list!". The local pub here claims that Walzing Matilda was sung here for the first time ever to a live gathering and of course, this is the birthplace of Qantas, the first commercial airline in the world. On the road now out of Winton to Longreach, Longreach is another historical town and I drive through to Emerald which is a lovely place and spent the night there. Off to Rockhampton, coast to coast how good is that. Gave the Delica a pat, she badly needs a wash, promised her a new set of shock absorbers as she is sitting very low on the back end. Told her not to get carried away, we must get home so don't relax. I will give her a good check up as well as a suspension lift when we get to Noosa. Rockhampton is a city and I was surprised at how big it is. I'll rest here for two days.

I'm now on my way to Maryborough, I left Graeme in the motel by mistake, they will find his photo and wonder who he is. Rockhampton is a lovely small city and I'm sure Graeme will be happy there. It has a big river called the Fitzroy, you can fish in it and camp out. Staying in a motel is not his cup of team. Maryborough is a nice large town and scenery in this part of Queensland is fantastic. On my way to Noosa now to meet up with my sister Lea and brother in law Keith. There is lots of traffic, big transports, etc. Prefer to drive in the desert than on this highway.

I met up with Lea and Keith at Cooroy, just out of Noosa and we had a cup of coffee at the local RSL, then off to see the 4WD man to look after the Delica for a new suspension. They ordered the parts and booked her in for later in the week. Lea and Keith lived in Peregian Springs, an estate on a lovely golf course community. Luxury living here and I'm in my element. We met Glen and her husband Murray in Cottontree which is about ten kms from Lea's house in Peregian, they have an apartment there and also one in Melbourne and spend four months in each place and travel overseas the rest of the time. News from home is not good, Gaye has broken her arm. Lisa is going down for the weekend and will take Mitzy back with her.

We were up early at 4.30 am and on our way to the Daintree in North Queensland. It will take us four days, maybe three with a bit of luck but we won't be hurrying. It's about the journey, not the destination. Lea and Keith are in their own car and they will travel with me to Port Douglas and then leave me to go back to Noosa. I will then be on my way with still half of my trip to go. The first stop is Mackay, a reasonably large city. Then Bowen, a typical Queensland town that gained recognition as the Darwin town in the film Australia.

We're on our way to Cardwell which is a lovely seaside town and staying in a motel with lovely view. We had fish and chips brought from a shop run by the biggest character you could ever come across. Ma Kettle I called her and she called me a "know all". Having owned a seafood takeaway and cafe I know it all regarding fish and chips. Still we entertained the customers with our banter.

Then off to Proserpine and Airlie Beach. Met up with an old friend Frances Johnson, she was Gaye's best mate growing up as early teenagers in Preston and I hadn't seen her for fifty years. We had lunch in Proserpine together, where she runs a florist shop. Earlier on we had visited her partner, John in their house in Airlie Beach. John runs a charter yacht business there. He seems a nice guy but a bit of a wheeler and dealer. Fran was sweet and much the same as I remembered her. We then moved onto Port Douglas, the scenery gets better and better. Palm trees and gardens by the roadside, it is stunning, I am so glad I decided to come to North Queensland. We pass through two big cities, well big by Australian standards, Townsville and Cairns. They are both very tropical and modern with lots of traffic. I got lost in Townsville but by GPS navigator got me back on track.

We arrived in Port Douglas and we're staying a Rydges resort with an apartment each. Very luxurious, but not a lot of people staying here, I think it must be the recession. Port Douglas is made up of mainly large resorts and shops, paradise for the females but good for us blokes too. We spent a day at the Daintree and Cape Tribulation, nearly at the top of North East Australia. I come from Augusta, the furthest South West point of Australia, this is just awesome!! The Daintree is amazing, could not describe it and do it justice. Getting a bit touristy but very well done and the nature side is well protected. It was a great day with a ferry crossing at the Daintree River. Mountains with mist on them, tropical jungles, flower, palm trees, mountain streams, it's got the lot. I'm off tomorrow on my way home. Lea and Keith will come part of the way, then I'm on my own. I'll miss them but I get the feeling that they'll enjoy a bit of peace and quiet as I talk a lot. Mostly about nothing but we live on opposite sides of Australia and it's not often we get together for any length of time. Somehow I guess they will miss me too.

We're off to Ravenshoe, Queensland's highest town. It's on my way home. Lea and Keith decide to come with me and stay overnight as it is also on their way. They can take a detour and it won't be far out of their way. There's lots of gorgeous tree kangaroos on this road and the visitor centre in Ravenshoe has won awards for their display of local fauna and aboriginal artefact, all original and dating back to the start of civilisation. If you're ever in Ravenshoe, visit this visitors centre, it's great.

I say goodbye to Lea and Keith and I'm on my way. The night before we'd a lovely dinner at the local hotel, we were the only people eating dinner, but the lovely hosts and hostesses made a great big fire and we sat by that and had our dinner. It is cold in Ravenshoe at this time of the year I can tell you but it was a very nice warm welcome. I had a strange experience one night in Port Douglas, I woke up at about 12.00 midnight and had a panic attack, I felt very anxious and vulnerable. I'd never felt like this before and I hope I never feel like it again. Maybe it was to do with leaving Lea and Keith and being back on my own again, I don't know, maybe mixed up with Graeme as well, I do know it was very scary and I don't want it to happen again. I had to take a sleeping pill and sat up and watched TV until I fell asleep. I woke up in the morning as good as gold, back to my old self. But it gave me an insight into how some people live their lives every day, lonely, anxious and with depression.

Anyway, I'm now off to Georgetown an old gold mining town. Not much there, I stayed overnight and moved onto Normanton on the Gulf of Carpentaria. This is a real Wild West town, there were even cowboys on horseback herding cattle on the outskirts of town. I crossed two massive rivers, the Gilbert and the Norman, both only had a trickle of water but in the wet season they run at between 150 metres and maybe kilometres wide.

Victoria had black Saturday in January 2009 and Normanton had rain like never seen before. The road into town was flooded for a stretch of kilometres. The town was isolated for 12 weeks, even the airstrip which is a base for over 10 flying doctor aircraft was under water. Hard to imagine it today as it is hot and dusty. This is the cool, dry season but it is hot, very hot. I called into the local pub for a beer and hopefully some lunch. It is called the Purple Pub and is an eye opener, very old and not much maintenance. It was opened in 1887. If you every go to Normanton, call in there, it's mainly run by aboriginals and I was the only white person at the time but that didn't bother me except for the fact that they only serve lunch now and again, maybe some Saturdays, maybe not. I had a beer and was on my way.

I did visit Karumba which is just up the road some 70 kms or so, it was a bitumen road to there and it is right on the water at the bottom of the Gulf of Carpentaria. A lot of tourists and caravans, this is about as far as they can go because after that you're on the dirt road but it is supposed to be the prawning and Barramundi capital of Australia. I was off early to Burketown the next day, this is a dirt road and it goes to the back of beyond, across some huge rivers although once again it was the dry season so there was no real worry. I met a lovely young French couple at a water crossing, she wanted to see a crocodile but was terrified to cross the creek. Being a brave Aussie, I went first, it was my first water crossing but I pretended to know what I was doing. I was a hero for a while and relieved that the Delica didn't sink. I had just taken pictures of a big crocodile in Normanton, the biggest ever caught in the world, 8.6 metres long and I was a little edgy I must admit.

The road wasn't too bad, I'd had far worse coming through central Australia. This is cattle country and you drive right through the open paddocks with thousands of cattle. They are well behaved and don't do anything silly. Lots of eagles feeding on bush pigs killed, I suspect, by trucks. Burketown is nothing to rave about, a pub, a store, a few houses, very hot and one would have to be hardy to live there. It's hard to imagine that Burke and Wills travelled through here by foot all those years ago. The vast distance with big rivers, crocodiles, hot as hell, they certainly deserve to be legends. Tomorrow I head to a place called Hells Gate, I can hardly wait. I'm spending the night there as the next town is a long way away in the Northern Territory. I'm feeling good now that it was cooled off. The sun here is very strong and it's hard to believe that home is having bad storms. Gaye said it has rained all but a few days since I left. We need the rain in the West and it looks like we are getting it. Hells Gate—I wonder what awaits me there!!

I'm on the road to Hells Gate—well named, worst road imaginable. Sand, rocks, corrugations, it's got it all. I worked out how to drive in these conditions, you put full power on and go for it. Don't drive too fast as you have to be ready for anything. Drop into a bulldust hole or dry creek crossing at 80kms per hour and its all over. Go too slow at 60 kms and you get shaken to pieces. Anyway, Hells Gate, it's a dead loss. A roadhouse and caravan park all locked up and deserted, no signs or notices to say why. Luckily myself and some other travellers that had pulled up had fuel. "Be ready for anything" seems to be the rule out here. Scenery is to be seen to be believed. Pity I have to watch the road and focus, as a lot of beautiful ranges and granite outcrops are missed.

I stop at most of the major rivers as you have to stop to size it all up. The rivers are massive, miles across and as I've said before, in the wet season you wouldn't be able to drive these roads. I came across lots of wild horses, some looked like good racing stock. Could there be a champion amongst them? I'd like to buy a horse when I get back, I've got that bug again. It was always Graeme's dream to get back into racing.

I arrive at Borroola, an aboriginal settlement and this is where I'll spend the night. The girl at reception looked just like Lisa. She had a beautiful smile so I told her so. She replied that it must be the ultimate compliment to be told you look like someone's daughter. She'd be right. There was a caravan enclosure where I'm going to spend the night. Borroola is purely aboriginal, it seems like a nice little settlement although some people say that there's usually a lot of trouble there. There are two service stations there, I went to the wrong one and they charged about double the price for diesel.

We're on the bitumen again and the Delica is in seventh heaven. I had to put her back together again at Borroola as she was battered and bruised but still going strong. She's purring along on the bitumen and I've promised her a wash as soon as possible.

I stopped at Cape Crawford for coffee at the Heartbreak Hotel which was Elvis themed. Here was a rip-off as well, it was over $2 a litre for diesel which was even more expensive than Borroola. I was warned by a grey nomad not to buy fuel here so I was prepared. Grey nomads are a good source of information but you have to pick the right ones. If they have a bushy beard and a wild look in their eye they are trustworthy.

I called back home to speak to Lisa and she said that Mitzy was very happy and it's obvious that Lisa has fallen under Mitzy's spell and I'm going to have trouble getting her back again. Mitzy won't go outside as the weather is cold and hence she has a toilet problem. Lisa says she will whip her into shape but my money is on Mitzy.

Gaye is still having problems with her arm and has a new cast on it. She also has a tooth problem. Gaye may not have the best teeth in the world but she must have close to the most expensive. I'll be home in about three weeks so hopefully she can hold together until then.

I'm driving into Daly Waters, its a skinny bitumen road and about 100 kms out of town I am waved down by a guy on the side of the road. It turns out it is Jerome, my old French pal. No trouble, he just saw me coming and as we hadn't seen each other for a couple of days, just wanted to catch up. Judy, his girlfriend, was sunbaking on top of the car. Her name's not Judy, it was some French name that I couldn't understand. Jerome speaks pretty good English, Judy's was hopeless. I decided not to give her a lecture and she probably wouldn't have understood anyway. The Northern Territory sun is so powerful she will just crisp up like a chicken, it's certainly not the French Riviera. Jerome doesn't seem to have much control over her but still they're having a ball. I met them again at Daly Waters Roadhouse a couple of hours later and we had lunch together, they were heading for Adelaide then home but Judy still hasn't seen a crocodile. She just wants to see one in the wild so they will go North for a few more days. I told them to go to WA, we have plenty of crocs there at the Malcolm Douglas Croc Park. They were a lovely couple and I should've got their contact details as my sister Lea is right into everything French and would no doubt have visited them. I wasn't to know this, but I was to go on a trip with Lea to Paris and maybe we could've met up with them. It was not to be however.

I am now in Katherine. Katherine is the Northern Territory's third largest town, although it's not all that big really. It's fairly modern and tropical of course and only about 250 kms from Darwin which is right up the top of Australia so I've travelled a fair way now. Katherine has a large Aboriginal population, mostly desert Aboriginals who live on the fringe of town. They are vastly different from the Aboriginals who live in the smaller communities such as Warburton and Borroloola or even Alice Springs. The Aborigines there seem more healthy and educated. Katherine's Aborigines are older, sad and downtrodden. It's very sad, they have a distant, sad look in their eyes as they shuffle from one street corner to the other. Most are alcoholics and now there are strict regulations on drink in these towns. I guess it has come a bit late for these people. If you are in your 40s or 50s I guess you haven't got long to live, that seems to be their reality. These Aboriginals don't speak English very well and prefer to speak their own language. They just seem to be hanging around outside the banks and waiting for their pensions and really it was very sad.

Leaving Katherine, I'm on the road to Kununurra, this road is very good. There were roadworks at Victoria River and the scenery here is fantastic. I'm looking forward to the Kimberley and the Victoria River is the start. Giant red granite cliffs and gorges and the Victoria River is massive with the road running alongside. The Roadhouse at Victoria River is neat and clean with a nice caravan park, I stopped for coffee and then continued onto Kununurra. This is by far the best town I've seen at the top end. It's clean, modern and very green and lush with wide streets. There's plenty of shade and smiles on everyone's faces. But then again, I'm back again in WA, what else would you expect. Queenslanders are friendly but I found Northern Territory people a bit standoffish and not enjoying life—maybe just my imagination?

I would live here in Kununurra, but certainly not in Katherine. Katherine was not for me—sad, hot and dusty. There are lots of grey nomads here and you can't blame them. They come up from the south where it is wet and cold. I've even been planning my next trip, next winter. Camping, fishing, exploring and seeing all the places I've missed. I would need twelve months to see everything, as it is I would've been away for about four months, not nearly long enough.

In Kununurra, I joined the Wilderness Society as they were having a recruitment drive as part of their protection of the Kimberley area. The next stop will be Halls Creek and then Fitzroy Crossing. This is the heart of the Kimberly and both towns have a bad reputation regarding the Aboriginal problem. I'm on the road to Fitzroy Crossing and it is a good road with lots of roadworks, new bridges being built over the big rivers and the scenery is living up to its reputation. Lots of ranges, red cliffs, green trees and grass—good cattle country and there are plenty of them, wild horses and a few roos but not much other life. Wild pigs are a problem and there are lots of them on the road as roadkill and there are eagles everywhere feeding on them. I stay overnight at Fitzroy Crossing in a safari tent. It was good fun, right on the banks of the mighty Fitzroy River.

I'm now on the road to Broome. Broome has lots of history, it's clean, modern and lots of things to do. I decided to book into an apartment and get a deal of three nights for the price of two. It would be a bit of luxury but I think Broome deserves three days. Broome was bombed in 1942 by the Japanese with loss of life and quite a few aircraft destroyed. My three days were well spent, I just about went everywhere, Cable Beach, travelled around the town doing what the locals do and went to Matso's Brewery. Tomorrow I'm off to Pardoo, this is just a roadhouse halfway between Broome and Port Hedland. I've been coast to coast and back again and tomorrow, I start my homeward run south down the coast. Back home in less than two weeks. Lisa wants me to stay for a few days in Perth with William and Peter while she and Paul go down south for a holiday. I'm looking forward to seeing the boys and catching up with Mitzy before I go back home to Augusta.

The Pardoo Roadhouse wasn't much I can tell you, I wasn't really impressed, you don't expect a lot from these places and I've been to some pretty small, rough roadhouses on my tour but I've never come across such grumpy people that were in the Pardoo roadhouse. The Sandfire Roadhouse which is just up the road was burnt to the ground recently and they were operating just out of a caravan but they were all smiles and couldn't do enough for me but Pardoo, I wasn't happy with them. They seemed to want to argue with me but anyway, as I'm writing this Cyclone Rusty is absolutely bombarding Pardoo and ripping it to shreds but I'd like to say to the Pardoo people this cyclone has got nothing to do with me, nothing whatsoever!

Off to Karatha now which was a real eye opener. It's a pretty big town with lots going on. I found it very hard to even get into a caravan park, all booked out. I went off to the port at Dampier to look at the ships going out and all the iron ore then I'm on my way through to Carnarvon through Geraldton and back home again.

It was great to just walk in, there was no-one home at Lisa's place, just Mitzy there by herself. She couldn't believe her eyes. She went ballistic and she looks really great. The only regret I have about the trip is that I couldn't have Graeme with me. This was devastating at first but somehow he seemed to be with me. It was scary at times but as the trip wore on it became more normal. I didn't reach the stage of talking to myself but sometimes I did talk to the Delica. This of course is normal, a man always talks to his car. Sometimes I may have been talking to Graeme, I don't really know. I wish that I could've spent more time with Glen and Murray, circumstances prevented that as they were going back to Melbourne I think. I spent a fair amount of time with Lea and Keith and that was great.

Graeme and Lisa panning for gold in Ballarat 1971

Graeme and Lisa at her house

CHAPTER 25

MOROCCO

After I returned from my Turkey trip, I really had the travel bug. My sister Lea was learning to speak French and she said "what about we go to Paris and spend a couple of weeks there?". I said "Yes, that would be nice but I would really like to go to somewhere more interesting. Paris would be nice but I was thinking more Morocco". She suggested we book a tour of Morocco, come back to Paris and spend maybe a week or ten days in Paris. It sounded good to me. She had a friend called Joan who would come with us. That was fine by me, the more the merrier.

We booked a 14 day Insight coach tour all around Morocco, we would then fly back to Paris. We had booked some boutique hotels, spending four or five days in one location, then go more or less south west to Givernny, where Monet the artist used to have his home and some lovely gardens. We booked a house on the internet which appeared to be in the country but turned out to be on a main road, still it was a nice house, centuries old and we had a good time there.

I was to leave from Perth Airport, Lea from Brisbane where she lived and Joan would leave from Melbourne, we would all meet up at the Singapore terminal and catch an Air France plane to Paris. From there we would fly to Casablanca and spent two days at the Sheraton Casablanca before the tour started. All in all it was about a 24 hour trip but it all went well. We met up and even though I'd never met Joan we got on well.

The two days that we spent at the Sheraton Casablanca were great because it gave us an insight into what Morocco was like. We explored all around the area by ourselves, it was a pretty seedy sort of an area but it was all part of the experience. We really enjoyed it. We then met the other tour group people, mostly Americans, but there were some Aussies, a nice couple, Wayne and Gina from Yunderup, we met them straight away and got on well. I was to have a bus companion called Hilda, a nice lady from New Jersey. We got on pretty well and she liked my sense of humour which was just as well otherwise I would've driven her crazy.

Everything was going well, the first stop was Rabat, the capital of Morocco and then we moved on to the desert to a town called Erfoud. We were on our way to Erfoud and must get there before sunset. So over the mountains we went, the little or medium Atlas Mountains, I'm not sure which. There are three Atlas Mountains, all the mountains in Morocco are called Atlas, some big and some not so big. We moved into semi-desert country where there were lots of oasis, not the puny ones you see in the movies, like a pond and a few palm trees, these stretched for miles, some had big houses on them as the people are quite wealthy. This is where most of the world's dates come from. We reached Erfoud, a hot, dusty, uninteresting town and we piled into a series of four wheel drives and out into the desert for about 50 kms, stopping to see how some Berbers live. We arrive at a type of resort where the camels are kept, my first thought was "Who would stay at a resort out here?", one day and the novelty would wear off.

We were allotted our camels, mine seems a little bit feisty but settled down after a stern word from his handler. We ride off into the sunset, it's been a cloudy day so there is no sun and the whole point of this is to see the sun set over the Sahara!! We reach our destination and sit on a sandune waiting for the sun to set. I think to myself "These people are waiting for a miracle." Everyone seemed disappointed and we waited until it was dark and then decide to go home. No sun, we hadn't seen it all day so it didn't set. But everyone had a good time.

I'm used to riding horses and I'm sure I'm blind from the sand blowing in my eyes. Lea is so excited so I try not to be a grouch, I just hope my eyesight is restored eventually. We drive back in the dark at what seems like 100 kms/hr. There was no road, just tracks, six or seven 4WDs racing each other over the desert. Two of our convoy break down so it was very late before we got back to the hotel.

The next stop after the desert town Erfoud was a city called Ouarzazate, it is the film capital of Morocco and heaps of famous desert movies have been made here, both American and French. The hotel was magnificent, it was all decked out in movie themes and there were lots of original props from some of the famous movies and they had the biggest swimming pool you are ever likely to see. Massive, you could've shot that Kevin Costner movie, Waterworld in the swimming pool it was that big. This city is also famous for its kasbah and castles, they are everywhere and you know what goes on in kasbahs, we all know that but if you don't, I'll tell you. Nothing, nothing at all, they are really just army barracks and fortresses built to stop the invaders coming from out of the desert, probably Berbers, although they are now quite good friends. They were probably used by the foreign legion as well so nothing goes on in the kasbahs which is a bit of a letdown.

Tomorrow we go to Marrakesh and to get there we must cross the high Atlas mountains and yes, they are high. Very dangerous and people live up there and even though it is summer there is still snow on the mountain. How they survive I've got no idea. Marrakesh is a good place with lots going on. Casablanca is probably the best known city in Morocco but not much goes on in Casablanca, although a famous movie was made there. We drive into Marrakesh down from the mountains and there was a beautiful freeway, miles long with tulips, roses, in fact all types of flowers, it was similar to the drive from Istanbul Airport where they had lots of tulips. This freeway was built by the King, they love their King here much like they used to love Ataturk in Turkey.

We spent the night before we were due to leave for Paris in Casablanca and I spent the whole night in the bathroom. I put it down to an upset stomach and still wasn't feeling very well when we had to get up early to catch our Paris flight, I hadn't slept at all but was hoping that I would soon start to feel better. Halfway through the flight which isn't a long one to Paris, I went to go to the toilet and woke up on the floor of the aircraft galley with a doctor trying to revive me. I had just passed out. I didn't know what was going on, they took me back to my seat and brought sister Lea up from the back of the aircraft where she was sitting with Joan. Not long after that I was violently ill, filling up a big black garbage back and finished up going into shock. On arrival at the airport they took me off the plane in a wheelchair, put me in an ambulance and took me to the airport hospital, where I was checked over and then taken off in an ambulance to the main Paris Hospital and finished up in the Emergency Department.

Lea and Joan checked in to the hotel and Lea came back to spend some time with me in the Emergency Department. They took lots of blood and samples and numerous tests, eventually giving me an intravenous antibiotic which I was allergic to so they stopped that and gave me another one which made me feel a bit better. After a couple of days I was discharged and Lea took me back to the hotel and shortly afterwards we headed down South to Givernny to our little holiday house that we'd booked.

I still wasn't feeling very well, but I was a lot better than I was. Lea and Joan went off exploring, they went to Monet's house and gardens, I stayed at home and went for a bit of a walk and didn't see much of this lovely little town.

We went back to Paris, I had an appointment at the hospital and was a day late for that because I couldn't speak French and couldn't understand the instructions. I was relieved that the Head of the Infectious Diseases at the hospital, a lovely Doctor, decided to give me some time, I think she was interested in my case. She checked me over, gave me more tests. We then we headed to the first hotel to pick up our luggage and go to the second hotel which was in a great location. I think it was on the West Bank but it was in the middle of where you want to be in Paris, near all the famous restaurants, boutiques, not far from the Luxembourg Gardens and right on the riverbank.

Our little hotel was virtually my home. Joan and Lea went off exploring, they did a tour around Paris, I would've loved to have gone but didn't really feel up to it. I hadn't eaten for quite a few days and was losing a bit of weight which I wasn't too worried about. We did go on a river trip however, we could walk to the river from our hotel which was great and from there we could see all the famous iconic places like the Eiffel Tower, the museums and galleries and the rest of it. I can remember it was quite a hot day, even though it was only the start of spring in Paris and I didn't feel particularly well but we enjoyed that.

Another thing we did a couple of days later was walk to the Luxembourg Gardens, this was great, all the famous statues were there that you see on famous movies and in magazines and to be there and actually see them live was great. We walked back to the hotel, we only had another day or so left in Paris.

My results had come through from the hospital. It turns out I had a very bad kidney infection but the antibiotics had started to work and the results were a lot better. Originally the Head of the Infectious Diseases Department said that if your kidneys don't improve it would be advisable for you not to fly and until we find out if this is what has caused the infection, you may be contagious. Anyway, there was an improvement with my kidneys which was great news. She did say that they were still very bad and I must go to my doctor as soon as I get back to Australia, have them tested again and if there was no further improvement, the worst case scenario was maybe a kidney transplant or maybe on a dialysis machine for the rest of my life. This was very frightening.

There was more to come however, we couldn't fly out because this was the time that the Iceland volcano had erupted and all flights out of Paris and this part of Europe were grounded. It looked like we would be stuck in this little hotel for quite some time. I wasn't concerned, we all had travel insurance and we were reassured that they would pay all our expenses, no-one could come into the hotel because there were no flights coming in so our rooms were safe, we would have somewhere to stay. As it turned out, Qantas started flying and we caught our regular flight out of Charles Du Gualle Airport.

It was great to get on that flight, hear the Aussie accents and when they asked me what I would like to eat, I didn't really know I hadn't eaten for a long time I said I don't really want anything maybe just a bread roll, they even found some vegemite to put on it for me. The flight home was great and I'm pleased to say I went to my doctor, had my kidneys checked and they are back to normal. This was all April 2010 and now in 2013 I've had quite a few tests done on my kidneys and they are all A1.

Paul Lisa Pete and Will

Young Pete scoops the pool in the Underage State Championships

Pete Surfing showing off his surfing manoeuvres

William in Action

Pete and Will, Silver Medals at the
2013 WA State Surf Life Saving Championship

Will and Pete Competing

Pete and Will at Rottnest Island, playing it cool

CHAPTER 26

MAURITIUS

I was back home again with good kidneys and my doctor was happy and said everything was OK and my kidneys were back to normal. So I thought another trip would be the go. I thought about Nepal, I'd made enquiries to a nice hotel in Kathmandu, run by an American lady, we went into quite a bit of detail about flights and what to do in Kathmandu and I ran it past my doctor. He said "no way, you're not going to Nepal. If you thought Morocco was bad, you'll find Nepal much, much worse and your kidneys cannot stand another hit. I'd forget about Nepal if I was you." OK, fair enough I would take an easier option and go to Mauritius. It sounded great, just a single flight over the Indian Ocean and I'd seen an advertisement in one of the travel sections of a nice little boutique hotel there. It turns out it was owned by a couple from Wagin in Western Australia. Anika, who was an accountant in Wagin, and her husband Chris had a farm there and they would fly backwards and forwards to their hotel. The hotel only catered for about 20 guests at any one time. I went in the off-season and as it turned out I was the only guest.

Chris and I had a lot in common, he's a little younger than me but he used to play for Subiaco and he was in the Police Force. He used to hang around Fremantle and Melville and we had a lot of mutual friends. I was accepted as one of the family. They told me good places to go and they had a taxi driver who virtually worked for the hotel and he picked me up at the airport and took me to the hotel. There are heaps and heaps of taxis in Mauritius so they're very competitive, you could book a taxi for the whole day for about $40 and it would take you wherever you wanted to go, they would stop and wait for you while you had lunch. If I went out of a night, they would pick me up from the hotel, take me to the restaurant, wait until I'd finished my meal, which could take 2-3 hrs, then drive me back to the hotel, all for about $10.

I had a really good time in Mauritius. It was great but we've got far better beaches in the South West. It was a nice place and it wasn't third world or anything like that. The Creole Indians there are fairly poor but nowhere near as poor as in some countries. There were a lot of French and English people and there was a good mixture of cultures and I had a great time.

Coming back home again, sister Glen said they were going on a cruise to New Zealand, would I like to join them. I decided I would as I'd never been on a cruise and it sounded like a fairly easy option. I flew to Melbourne and met up with Glen and Murray and away we went on the Dawn Princess. It was great, the first stop was the Milford Sound which was an unbelievable eye opener, around to Dunedin and up further to Christchurch. At Christchurch we did some shopping. It's a lovely place Christchurch, I'd been there before when we went on our New Zealand tour for the inter-dominion. We then went to Wellington and got sensational news, an earthquake had hit Christchurch and flattened it. It was only two days since we'd been there in the same place where everything was destroyed. We just couldn't believe it, we were so lucky and it was so sad for the people of New Zealand.

That was a great trip, the only big disappointment was not being able to meet up with good friends Merryn and Dave who I had met on my Turkey tour. We had arranged to meet and they were looking forward to showing us around their home town. They came to meet the ship but for some reason or other we missed each other.

I've since been on another trip on the Dawn Princess. I flew to Brisbane, once again met up with Glen and Murray and away we went around the top of Australia, to Airlie Beach, Port Douglas, Darwin, Broome, then off to Lombok, had some fairly good times there. Murray and I had a fight with a taxi driver over a fare but that wasn't a problem. They didn't put us in jail so we came through that OK. There were big storms along the West Coast so we didn't call into Geraldton but we got home safe and this was another lovely trip.

At home in my little blue house, life is good. Gaye has her ups and downs but is hanging in there. My life is very quiet these days. I spend a fair bit of time watching football on TV. I am a self-confessed football tragic as you've probably gathered throughout the book. I'm very passionate about the West Coast Eagles, I can't believe in my younger days I was completely besotted with Collingwood, I now hate them, nearly as much as I hate the Fremantle Dockers!

Anyway, I need to talk about my immediate family. I have said a fair bit about Graeme but not much about Lisa. I guess I'm leaving the best 'til last. Lisa has always been a quality person and along with Paul they have brought up their family in an excellent fashion. They have both led by example, been with the boys every step of the way. Lisa has always been involved with the boy's education, being on school committees and such like.

Walsh Family at Glen and Murray's house. Rene, Gavin with Dylan and Alana.

Holidaying in the snow

The Robertson Boys

The Wilmonts at home

The Armstrongs photo

Robertson Family with Michelle and her girls

William. Studying Hard

Will and Pete with their cousins, Ollie, Lloyd and Finny

William Competing

Pete takes on the men and wins Gold for WA

Both Lisa and Paul were heavily involved with the Surf Lifesaving Club, Age Managers, graduating through the Nippers and up to State level competitions. Lisa was first to do the Rottnest swim, setting a great example for William who has just done his first Rotto swim and performed magnificently. Peter will follow I'm sure in years to come. Talking of Peter, he has represented his school in both swimming and surfing, usually claiming gold. He has started his own business manufacturing surfboards. Paul has been a great inspiration in this, encouraging him all the way. Paul of course, surfs with the boys and has spent a lot of time paddling kayaks with them.

Lisa and Paul also run a successful business together and Lisa is a qualified personal trainer and is a great example everyone on how to live a healthy life. This year William competed for his State in Sydney at the Australian Surf Lifesaving Championships, Peter has also represented WA in previous year. Peter and William has a heap of school and club medals for all things performed in the water. They are both exceptional young men and I could not be more proud of them.

It's not just their sporting achievements that make them a great family. They are just nice, well adjusted citizens who love life.

I'm biased of course but when I look back to my parents I realise they just had great family values and this has flowed on. Both my sisters' families have similar values and this shows in their grandchildren. It may go right back to our Red Cliffs days, life was so simple, no drugs, no junk food and no big egos. I love my life here, my health is fine and without doubt Augusta is the best place in the world. People think it must be very cold as we are so far south. Let them believe this, we know differently, we have no traffic lights, no fast food outlets and most times, not many tourists, they usually stop at Margaret River which suits us, although I feel sorry for the businesses, some of them struggle a bit because of lack of numbers. My live-in companion is Mitzy and we look after each other. This is the end, but not the end of me!

Mitzy photo